The LEGO Arduino Cookbook

Expanding the Realm of MINDSTORMS EV3 Invention

Grady Koch

Apress®

The LEGO Arduino Cookbook: Expanding the Realm of MINDSTORMS EV3 Invention

Grady Koch
Yorktown, VA, USA

ISBN-13 (pbk): 978-1-4842-6302-0   ISBN-13 (electronic): 978-1-4842-6303-7
https://doi.org/10.1007/978-1-4842-6303-7

Managing Director, Apress Media LLC: Welmoed Spahr
Acquisitions Editor: Aaron Black
Development Editor: James Markham
Coordinating Editor: Jessica Vakili

Distributed to the book trade worldwide by Springer Science+Business Media New York, 1 NY Plaza, New York, NY 10014. Phone 1-800-SPRINGER, fax (201) 348-4505, e-mail orders-ny@springer-sbm.com, or visit www.springeronline.com. Apress Media, LLC is a California LLC and the sole member (owner) is Springer Science + Business Media Finance Inc (SSBM Finance Inc). SSBM Finance Inc is a Delaware corporation.

For information on translations, please e-mail booktranslations@springernature.com; for reprint, paperback, or audio rights, please e-mail bookpermissions@springernature.com.

Apress titles may be purchased in bulk for academic, corporate, or promotional use. eBook versions and licenses are also available for most titles. For more information, reference our Print and eBook Bulk Sales web page at http://www.apress.com/bulk-sales.

Any source code or other supplementary material referenced by the author in this book is available to readers on GitHub via the book's product page, located at www.apress.com/978-1-4842-6302-0. For more detailed information, please visit http://www.apress.com/source-code.

Printed on acid-free paper

Table of Contents

TABLE OF CONTENTS

About the Author

Grady Koch emphasizes building things from LEGO that can be applied to practical use in science, engineering, or security. He is the author of *High-Tech LEGO Projects, LEGO Wind Energy*, and *Secrets of Eli's LEGO Collection*. He also writes for and runs www.hightechlego.com, which features various LEGO technology projects. His day job since 1987 has been as a research engineer with NASA Langley Research Center. There, he works with technology for remote sensing atmospheric phenomena. He holds a PhD in Electrical Engineering. And he holds three patents in the field of wind measurements with lidar.

About the Technical Reviewer

Associate Professor **Gene Harding** has a Master of Science in Electrical Engineering from Rose-Hulman Institute of Technology. His experience includes 28 years of combined active and reserve service in the United States Air Force and 3 years in the private industry with Agilent Technologies. He has taught electrical engineering technology at Purdue's South Bend location since the fall of 2003.

Introduction

MINDSTORMS EV3 serves as an excellent platform for experimenting with robotics. And with a little push, given in this book, the use of the EV3 Intelligent Brick can be expanded to provide a means for rapid prototyping of all sorts of inventions. There are several single-board host computers for developing inventions, such as the Raspberry Pi, BeagleBone, or LattePanda. There are even hardware adapters to use MINDSTORMS motors on a Raspberry Pi or BeagleBone. But this book keeps LEGO as the foundation, including the MINDSTORMS EV3 Intelligent Brick as a host computer. There are several reasons for this LEGO-centric approach.

First, the mechanical design of inventions is simple by using the vast array of LEGO building bricks that can be attached to the EV3 Intelligent Brick. There's no need to build an enclosure around the computer heart, since the EV3 Intelligent Brick is already powered, hardened, and enclosed. It has built-in batteries, display, control buttons, speaker, and SD card storage. Mounting points on the rear and sides of the EV3 Intelligent Brick provide quick and easy attachment of sensors and motors.

Second, the artistic aspects of LEGO are maintained by using the EV3 Intelligent Brick as the host computer. LEGO constructions have an aesthetic appeal enjoyed by artists and builders, so the EV3 Intelligent Brick is used as the basis in this book. This artistic appeal is in contrast to the alternate approach of building a device from a Raspberry Pi and trying to put a LEGO box around the device, potentially resulting in a clumsy mash-up. In this book, LEGO is the heart of the invention.

Third, the educational foundation of LEGO can be built upon to introduce kids and students to more sophisticated technologies. LEGO adapts to kids' interests as they grow older, culminating with

MINDSTORMS EV3. As mastery of MINDSTORMS is achieved, this knowledge can be built upon to learn and use more complex electronic and software capabilities.

The key to expanding LEGO MINDSTORMS is introducing the wide selection of sensors, actuators, devices, and even smartphones that can be interfaced through an Arduino controller. This book shows how to add this Arduino interface for many applications. No prior knowledge of Arduino is required.

The development of this book's ideas begins in Chapter 1 with introducing the Arduino. Instructions are given on how to select among the many varieties of the Arduino, along with the accessories for attaching it to LEGO bricks and wire connections. Two options are suggested of either an Arduino Uno circuit board with shield accessories or the STEMTera. A design is given for mounting of the Arduino alongside the EV3 Intelligent Brick to create a LEGO workstation for building prototype inventions.

Chapter 2 discusses programming the EV3 Intelligent Brick, preparing to interface it to the Arduino. The MINDSTORMS EV3 programming environment will be used throughout this book, taking advantage of its likely familiarity with many readers. While prior experience working with the robots of the EV3 Home Edition software is helpful, it is not necessary to build the projects in this book with instructions given on how to get started and how to program the projects' EV3 code. Advanced programming blocks are used in some of the projects in this book that readers may not be familiar with, so these blocks are introduced in this chapter.

Chapter 3 sets up the Arduino, specifically in how to program this device and how to interpret the architecture of an Arduino program sketch. Arduinos are programmed with a variant of the C language, which can get complicated. However, programs are largely simplified by using sketches already developed and tested for a particular sensor or actuator. So an approach is taken in this book of using these predeveloped sketches, with some minor modifications. These modifications are documented throughout this book. All of the sketches found in this book can be downloaded from `www.github.com`.

Chapter 4 takes a look at the sensors available for projects. While Arduino-based sensors are the primary interest of this book, many of this book's projects combine Arduino sensors with LEGO-made sensors or motors, so an overview is given of MINDSTORMS-based devices. A motivation to consider Arduino sensors is the wide capability they offer, but a drawback of so much variety is trying to figure out which sensor will work. So Arduino sensors are classified in this chapter by how they interface with the Arduino, either by pulse-width modulation (PWM), inter-integrated circuit (I2C), or serial peripheral interface (SPI). Some project designs need electronic components to send signals between sensors, the Arduino, and the EV3 Intelligent Brick. Such connections can involve resistor and/or capacitor circuits, so a guide is presented on understanding and buying these components.

Chapter 5 describes the first project—a metal detector built from an electromagnetic inductive sensor. The EV3 Intelligent Brick sounds and flashes an alarm when a metal is nearby, with an indication also given of how far away the metal is from the sensor. This project is first built on the LEGO Arduino Workstation of Chapter 1 and then is built in an alternate form of a handheld metal detector. The sensor in this project communicates with the Arduino by I2C and then with an analog signal to the EV3 Intelligent Brick.

Chapter 6 reverses the direction of data flow of Chapter 5, by now having the EV3 Intelligent Brick generate an analog signal that is read by the Arduino. The Arduino then sends I2C commands to the external device of a linear array of color-programmable light-emitting diodes (LEDs). Various LED color patterns can be displayed, useful for adding lighting effects to LEGO models.

Chapter 7 delves more deeply into I2C communication, a powerful tool for sending and receiving data to or from the EV3 Intelligent Brick. The

I2C passes data in 7-bit words, so a description is given on how decimal numbers are represented in this digital format. I2C communication, facilitated by a programming block developed by Dexter Industries, works within the EV3 programming environment to keep programs simple. The software interface for the Arduino end of I2C is also developed and explained in this chapter.

The I2C capability built in the previous chapter is exploited in Chapter 8 to combine a lidar with LEGO inventions. The lidar can measure target distance up to 40 m, reporting results to the EV3 Intelligent Brick for a variety of possible uses. Example applications are shown in a scanning lidar for profiling an outdoor area, as well as measuring the height and canopy thickness of a tree. Scanning is accomplished by mounting the lidar on a LEGO EV3 Large Motor. Further capability is added by combining a camera with the scanning lidar, with an example project of monitoring roadway traffic. The data communication link between the Arduino and the lidar is by PWM.

Chapter 9 explores the use of sensors that communicate by SPI, in this case a weather sensor of temperature, barometric pressure, and humidity. Another environmental measurement is added by use of a LEGO EV3 Color Sensor to record the ambient light level. The EV3 Intelligent Brick logs these four meteorological parameters over the course of many hours. An example project is shown of how weather parameters vary over the course of a few days.

Chapter 10 introduces working with Arduino shields, which offer more sophisticated functionality than the discrete sensors used in earlier chapters. The shield used in this chapter is a spectrum analyzer that separates audio or music signals into several frequency bands. This spectral data is read by the EV3 Intelligent Brick in an example project to visually and mechanically represent the frequency content of music. The seven spectral bands are displayed in a bar graph format on an LED array. Also, three of the spectral bands are used to drive three different LEGO mechanisms that dance in time with music.

Whereas the previous chapter has the EV3 Intelligent Brick receiving data from an Arduino shield, Chapter 11 has the EV3 Intelligent Brick sending data to an Arduino shield. The shield used in this chapter is a vibrant two-dimensional LED display with a color adjustable by the user to contemplate their favorite color. Color adjustment is made by LEGO EV3 motors adapted to serve as control knobs for setting the levels of red, green, and blue constituent colors that get mixed together.

Chapter 12 features an Arduino shield that interfaces with a smartphone for a wide range of applications. The communications, imaging, and sensing capabilities of a smartphone can be incorporated into LEGO inventions. Two example projects are described. First, a smartphone's orientation sensor provides data to the EV3 Intelligent Brick, which in turn orients the tilt of a LEGO liftarm to match the smartphone's angle. The second project is a security monitor that uses an EV3 Ultrasonic Sensor to trigger the smartphone to take a picture and send email notification that an intruder has been detected.

Each project in this book is described with step-by-step instructions for the building aspects involved: LEGO part assembly, electronics, wiring, EV3 code, and Arduino sketch. All the parts used in a chapter are summarized in an appendix, along with suggested sources for purchasing electronic components. LEGO parts are also identified in each chapter with a graphical parts diagram that also gives the part's name and number so it can be found on LEGO part supply sources such as Bricklink (www.bricklink.com).

CHAPTER 1

The LEGO Arduino Workstation

A wide new range of LEGO inventions can be realized by combining MINDSTORMS with an Arduino. Arduino is a single-board host controller for many types of sensors, motors, displays, actuators, and interfaces. It has become the most common host controller for electronics developers due to its low cost and ease of use. The Arduino is meant for nonexpert electronics builders to be able to build their own inventions. In this chapter, the hardware for connecting MINDSTORMS EV3 with an Arduino will be developed. This LEGO Arduino Workstation serves as a platform for building the projects found in this book.

The Arduino

The Arduino controller comes in many versions that can be confusing to distinguish from one another. This book uses the basic workhorse version known as the Arduino Uno, shown in Figure 1-1. The LEGO Arduino has many connection points for power and signal input and output that will be used throughout this book. Most of the connection points are by the rows of pins, called *headers*, on top of the device. Labels on the circuit board and on the side of the headers indicate, in abbreviated form, what these pins do. Other connections on the circuit board are for power input and a micro-USB connector for programming the Arduino Uno. These connections will be discussed in the following chapters.

© Grady Koch 2020
G. Koch, *The LEGO Arduino Cookbook*, https://doi.org/10.1007/978-1-4842-6303-7_1

Figure 1-1. *The Arduino Uno is a programmable board for hosting sensors and controllers*

In this chapter, the mechanical mounting and interface of the Arduino Uno to LEGO are built. Standing alone, as in Figure 1-1, the Arduino Uno is inconvenient to connect to LEGO. So a mechanical mounting plate can be purchased from the 3D printing marketplace that fits in the four mounting holes of the Arduino Uno. Such a plate is shown in Figure 1-2, purchased from `www.shapeways.com`.

Figure 1-2. *Connecting the Arduino Uno to LEGO involves a baseplate for a mechanical interface (at the left) and an electrical interface (at the right)*

In addition to a baseplate for the mechanical interface of the Arduino to LEGO, an electrical interface is needed to connect power and signals between the Arduino and the EV3 Intelligent Brick. This electrical interface is conveniently implemented with a breadboard, a device used for building prototype electronic circuits. Wires and the leads of electronic components slide into the holes of the breadboard to connect circuits. An Arduino-connected breadboard is available in the form of the Proto Shield, such as the one pictured in Figure 1-2. The Proto Shield has pins on the bottom that match the headers on the Arduino, and the connection between the two is made by pressing the Proto Shield into the Arduino's headers. The assembled three components of baseplate/Arduino/Proto Shield are shown in Figure 1-3. Also shown in Figure 1-3 is an alternative Arduino implementation, known as a STEMTera. The STEMTera is a combined breadboard and Arduino Uno—the Arduino is encased in the base of the breadboard. In addition, the STEMTera has a LEGO-compatible mechanical mounting on the bottom of the device, so it can simply be pressed together with LEGO parts. Throughout this book, the STEMTera version is used for two reasons: (1) the STEMTera costs less than the baseplate/Arduino/Proto Shield approach, and (2) the STEMTera is more rugged and more attractive.

Figure 1-3.   *Two possible Arduino implementations are the STEMTera (at the left) and a stack of a 3D printed adapter, Arduino Uno, and Proto Shield*

Assembling the LEGO Arduino Workstation

A LEGO platform can be built to hold the EV3 Intelligent Brick, Arduino, and various prototype setups. Such a platform is shown in Figure 1-4, based on 12×24 bricks. Building instructions follow Figure 1-4.

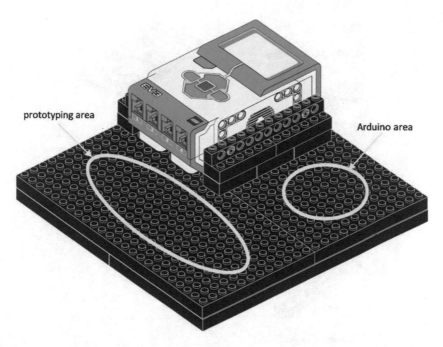

Figure 1-4. *The LEGO Arduino Workstation includes the EV3 Intelligent Brick, Arduino, and area for attachment of experimental prototypes*

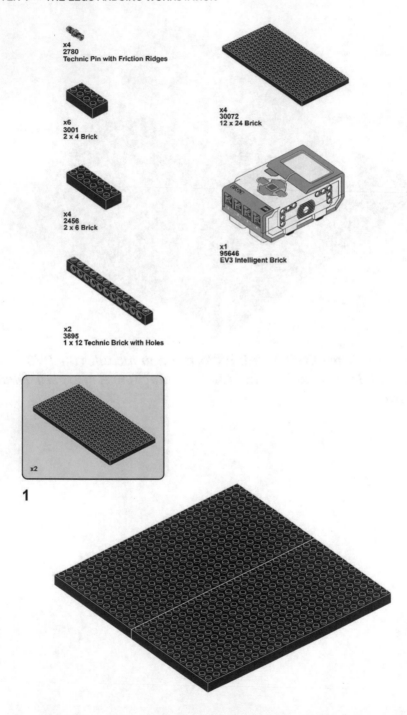

x4
2780
Technic Pin with Friction Ridges

x6
3001
2 x 4 Brick

x4
2456
2 x 6 Brick

x2
3895
1 x 12 Technic Brick with Holes

x4
30072
12 x 24 Brick

x1
95646
EV3 Intelligent Brick

x2

1

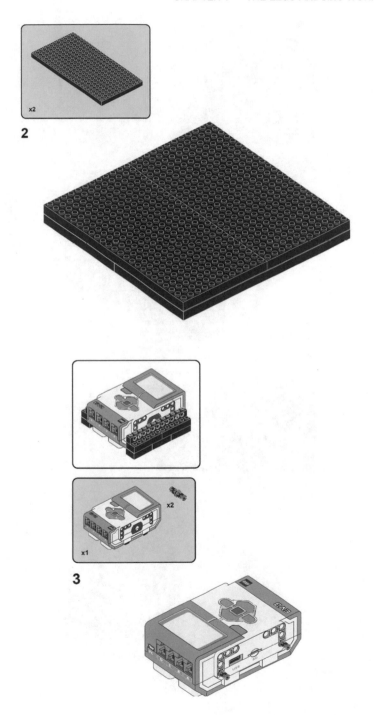

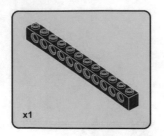

4

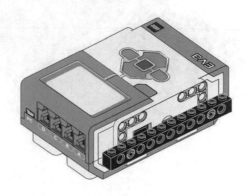

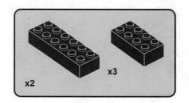

5

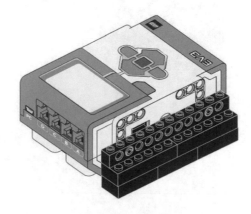

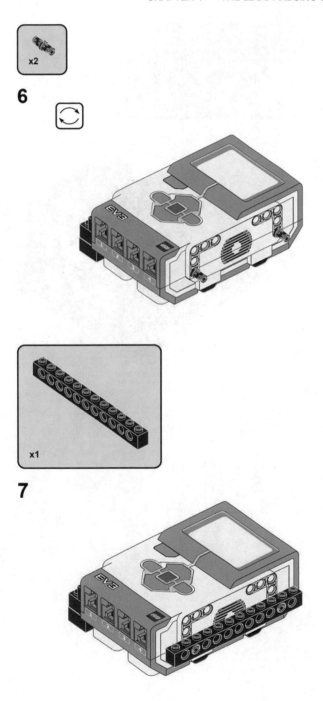

6

7

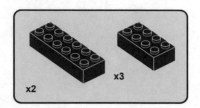

8

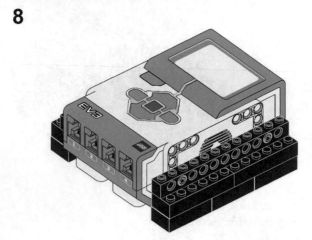

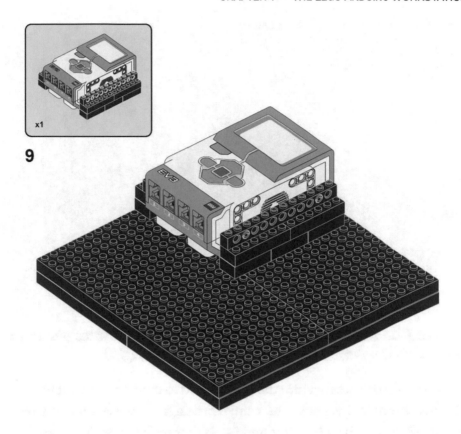

The Breadboard and Wiring

A feature of the LEGO Arduino Workstation is a breadboard for making electronic connections. One set of connections that needs to be made is to the EV3 Intelligent Brick, which can be accomplished with a Breadboard Connector Kit available from Mindsensors.com shown in Figure 1-5. An EV3 cable goes between the EV3 Intelligent Brick and this Breadboard Connector. The Breadboard Connector has a male header of pins that can be pressed into the breadboard of the LEGO Arduino Workstation.

Figure 1-5. *The Breadboard Connector Kit comes in three pieces (at the left) that have to be soldered together (at the right)*

Wires can be pressed into the breadboard to connect the various circuits shown in this book. There are two designs of these jumper wires to consider: straight solid wires and flexible stranded wires. These two types of jumper wires are pictured in Figure 1-6. While either type of wire could be used in the projects of this book for connecting two points on a breadboard, straight solid wires will more often be seen in projects of this book because they are less easily pulled loose than the looping connections of flexible stranded wires.

Figure 1-6. *Wire connections can be made with jumper wires of two styles: straight solid wires that lay flat against the breadboard (at the left) or flexible stranded wires (at the right)*

Final Assembly

A completed LEGO Arduino Workstation is shown in Figure 1-7, in which both the EV3 Intelligent Brick and STEMTera Arduino are attached to the LEGO baseplate. The Breadboard Connector has been pressed into place, with an EV3 cable connected between the breadboard and the EV3 Intelligent Brick.

Figure 1-7. *The assembled LEGO Arduino Workstation is ready for project development*

Summary

This chapter introduced the Arduino Uno that will be used throughout the book. The Arduino Uno needs accessories to work with LEGO projects, including a mounting plate and breadboard. These accessories can be stacked together for a compact solution. An alternate Arduino solution was presented in the form of a STEMTera breadboard, which has an Arduino Uno embedded in the base of a breadboard. A platform was presented to build projects on, called the LEGO Arduino Workstation. The LEGO Arduino Workstation holds the EV3 Intelligent Brick, Arduino, and an area for building LEGO-based prototypes. An electronic link between the EV3 Intelligent Brick and the Arduino was designed in the form of a Breadboard Connector. Now that the hardware has been gathered into a compact package, the next chapter moves on to aspects of software programming.

CHAPTER 2

Programming the EV3 Intelligent Brick

A quick overview of the essential steps is presented in this chapter for programming in the MINDSTORMS EV3 environment. After this overview, some of the more advanced programming techniques will be presented that are used in this book including My Blocks and working with third-party developed programming blocks. While there are many programming languages that have been adapted to work with MINDSTORMS, the programming for the EV3 Intelligent Brick used in this book stays with the simple graphical-based environment supplied by LEGO.

Getting Started with the MINDSTORMS EV3 Programming Environment

The MINDSTORMS EV3 program, which can be downloaded at `www.lego.com/en-us/themes/mindstorms/download`, associated with the LEGO 31313 set has the welcome lobby screen shown in Figure 2-1. This screen comes up when the program is started. Beginners are meant to click one of the five robots in the lobby to learn to build and activate a particular robot. But to create a MINDSTORMS EV3 program from scratch, the option is selected from the toolbar at the top of the screen for File ➤ New Project.

© Grady Koch 2020
G. Koch, *The LEGO Arduino Cookbook*, https://doi.org/10.1007/978-1-4842-6303-7_2

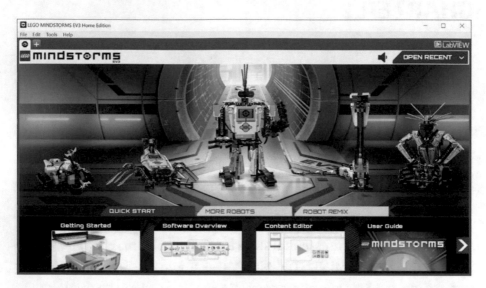

Figure 2-1. *The welcome lobby screen of the MINDSTORMS EV3 program has options for basic tutorials, as well as creating custom programs*

This brings up a programming screen, shown in Figure 2-2. At this point, it's a good idea to check for a connection to an EV3 Intelligent Brick, which can be determined at the bottom-right section of the screen. Figure 2-2 shows a situation in which an EV3 Intelligent Brick is not found, as indicated by the message "No Brick Connected."

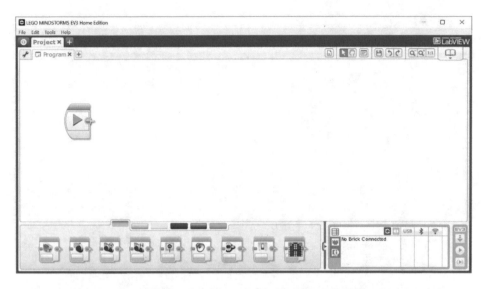

Figure 2-2. *Programs are built in the MINDSTORMS EV3 programming environment by dragging various blocks onto the center section of the screen*

There are three ways to connect the EV3 Intelligent Brick to the host programming computer: USB cable, Bluetooth, or WiFi. The USB connection is the simplest, using the cable supplied with the MINDSTORMS EV3 31313 set. The Bluetooth or WiFi connection allows loading programs without a cable, though requiring some setup as described at www.lego.com/en-us/service/help/products/themes-sets/Mindstorms. These wireless connections can be useful if the USB cable is not at hand. Bluetooth is easier to set up than WiFi, since WiFi requires purchasing a separate dongle. When the EV3 Intelligent Brick is connected to the host computer, it will show up as found in the lower-right corner, such as in the case of Figure 2-3 where a USB cable connection has been made. Of course, for the EV3 Intelligent Brick connection to be made, the brick must be turned on, which is accomplished by pressing the center button on the front panel.

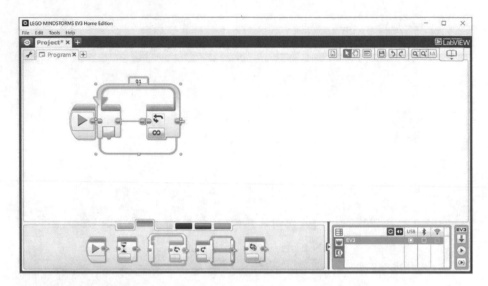

Figure 2-3. *Connection to the EV3 Intelligent Brick is confirmed in the lower right-hand corner of the programming environment*

Programming

Programs are created by placing programming blocks in the center of the screen, as has been done in Figure 2-3, with the insertion of a Loop block. Programming blocks are organized under tabs at the bottom of the screen, with selection of a particular block made by a click-hold-drag into the programming area. Tabs are under six headings, as labeled in Figure 2-4. An example programming step is taken in Figure 2-4 with selection of a Medium Motor block from the Action tab being inserted into the loop.

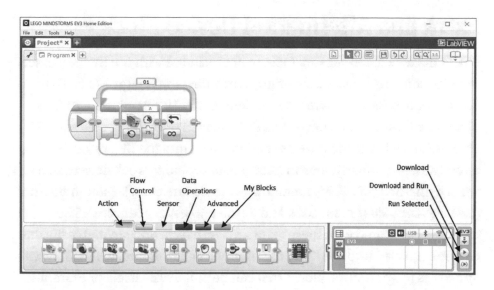

Figure 2-4. *Programming blocks are organized by function under tabs at the bottom of the screen*

EV3 code diagrams are part of the project chapters that follow in this book and can be duplicated by pulling in the matching blocks and selecting the options on each block. Or the programs can be downloaded from `www.github.com` to be imported into the EV3 programming environment. Once the program has been written, it gets downloaded for execution to the EV3 Intelligent Brick by one of the three buttons at the bottom right of the screen: "Download," "Download and Run," or "Run Selected." "Download" places the program into the memory of the EV3 Intelligent Brick, but does not run the program. To run the program, the center button on the EV3 Intelligent Brick is pressed. This download-only option is useful for a situation in which some action of the program, like activation of a motor, needs to be watched closely for proper operation. If no problems are anticipated, then "Download and Run" can be selected as a shortcut to both place the program into memory and run the program. The last option of "Run Selected" is a tool for debugging in which only the code blocks highlighted by mouse selection are run.

Extra and Aftermarket Device Blocks

LEGO makes several sensors that are not included with the EV3 31313 set but that can be purchased separately, including the Energy Meter, Gyro Sensor, Sound Sensor, Temperature Sensor, and Ultrasonic Sensor. The blocks for these sensors have to be downloaded (`www.lego.com/en-us/ themes/mindstorms/downloads`) and installed into the EV3 programming environment. Similarly, aftermarket sensor developers sell devices that will work with MINDSTORMS, including Mindsensors.com, Dexter Industries (`www.dexterindustries.com`), and Vernier (`www.vernier.com`). The websites associated with these extra sensors have a downloadable file that can be imported into the EV3 programming environment, where they will appear as programming blocks that can be pulled into use. For example, Figure 2-4 has two programming blocks under the Action tab that are extra devices for a Dexter Industries dSwitch and a Mindsensors LED Matrix. The installation of these programming blocks is done from the toolbar by selecting Tools ➤ Block Import. A prompt will then appear to find the .ev3 file from where it was stored after download from the sensor developer's website.

My Blocks

The MINDSTORMS programming environment has an advanced feature to collect groups of coding blocks under a single block, similar to programming a subroutine in line-by-line coding. This single-block representation, called *My Blocks*, is useful when the same section of code is used repeatedly. Figure 2-5 serves as an example to show how My Blocks are created. As in Figure 2-5, the sections of code blocks to collect together are highlighted, in this example, to play a tone, create a random number, display the number, and pause for 1 second. Highlighting the blocks is done by left-click and hold, then drawing a box around the section of blocks. Alternatively, multiple blocks can be selected by holding down the Shift key and left-clicking individual blocks. Highlighted blocks appear with a blue border around them. The Start block is never part of a My Block creation, so it is not highlighted in the example of Figure 2-5.

Figure 2-5. *Blocks to include in a My Block are first highlighted*

After the blocks of interest have been highlighted, My Block construction is initiated from the toolbar with selection of Tools ➤ My Block Builder. A menu then appears, such as that in Figure 2-6. Attributes get assigned to the new My Block, including Name, Description, and Icon. In the example of Figure 2-6, the icon of a die has been selected to represent the My Block. Clicking Finish in the My Block Builder will bring back the program area of the screen, as shown in Figure 2-7, and a result of the programming blocks previously highlighted being replaced with the new My Block. Much like any other programming block, the new My Block can be used again as many times as desired by selecting it from under the My Blocks tab.

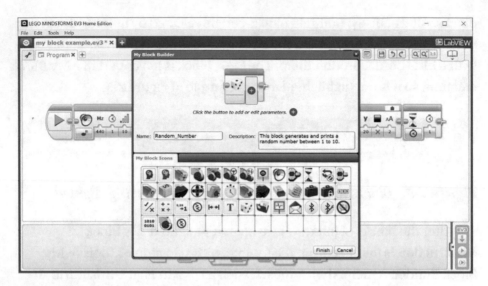

Figure 2-6. *Opening the My Block Builder provides areas for user input for name, description, and icon*

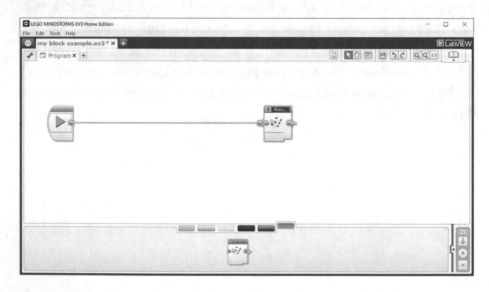

Figure 2-7. *The new My Block can be pulled into action by selecting it from the My Blocks tab*

Summary

This chapter reviewed the setup for the software programming of the EV3 Intelligent Brick. The EV3 Intelligent Brick is programmed by a graphical user interface, assembling various control blocks to create programs. A more advanced use of the EV3 programming environment was introduced with the means to import control blocks that are not part of the core EV3 programming environment. Importing control blocks is associated with both LEGO and aftermarket devices, such as will be found in later chapters of this book. Another advanced feature explored was the creation of My Blocks, user-made subroutines useful for when a set of program blocks will be used repeatedly.

CHAPTER 3

Programming the Arduino

In this chapter, a guide is presented on a quick start to programming the Arduino, including how to install the Arduino programming environment, connect the Arduino Uno board to a host computer, and understand the basic structure of an Arduino program. The Arduino has a vast capability, and programming can get rather sophisticated. Many books have been written on programming the Arduino, ranging in skill level from beginner's guides for students to advanced applications for professional engineers. However, the description in this chapter is rather simple, with the intent to understand just enough about programming to get the Arduino working in LEGO-based designs. The Arduino programs, called *sketches*, used throughout this book are adapted from various manufacturers of sensors and devices, who provide sketches specifically for their products. It's sufficient to simply learn the rudiments of Arduino programming so that these premade sketches can be put to use.

Installing the Arduino Integrated Development Environment (IDE)

The Arduino programming utility is called Integrated Development Environment (IDE), with options available for Windows, Mac OS, and Linux operating systems. Download of the IDE can be found at

© Grady Koch 2020
G. Koch, *The LEGO Arduino Cookbook*, https://doi.org/10.1007/978-1-4842-6303-7_3

www.Arduino.cc/en/Main/Software, such as in the screenshot of Figure 3-1. Upgrades are released every few months to the IDE, as identified by the version number, such as version 1.8.12 seen in Figure 3-1. Most of these upgrade changes are rather minor, with no effect on high-level programming used throughout this book.

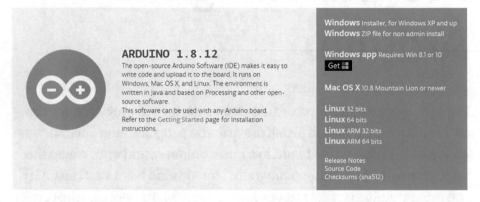

Figure 3-1. *The download page for the Arduino IDE shows options for several host computer operating systems*

Navigating the Arduino IDE

Opening the IDE will bring up a work area, as pictured in the screenshot of Figure 3-2. The large area in the center of the IDE is for the development of sketches with two sets of commands, as noted in the comments on the IDE screen: the setup for programming commands that run once and loop for commands that run in a continuous repetition. The IDE also includes utilities for saving and downloading sketches onto the Arduino board, as described in the following sections.

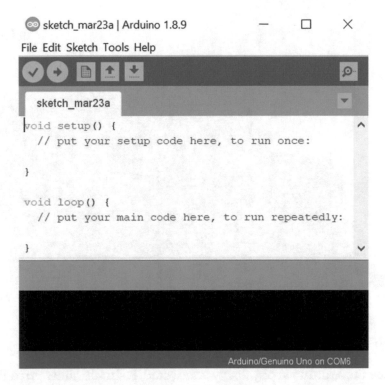

Figure 3-2. *The IDE provides for the development of sketches and their download to the Arduino*

The first tab to consider from the toolbar is Tools, after connecting the Arduino board to the host computer by a USB cable. Figure 3-3 shows the micro-USB connection on the Arduino board, using a STEMTera board as an example.

Figure 3-3. *Connection of the Arduino to a host computer is by a USB connection*

Once the Arduino is physically connected, it should show up in the IDE under Tools ➤ Port, as pictured in Figure 3-4. The Arduino is recognized by the Arduino/Genuino Uno name following the assigned Port. A further diagnostic on a correct connection can be found under Tools ➤ Get Board Info, with a positive result being a pop-up screen showing addresses and serial number associated with the Arduino.

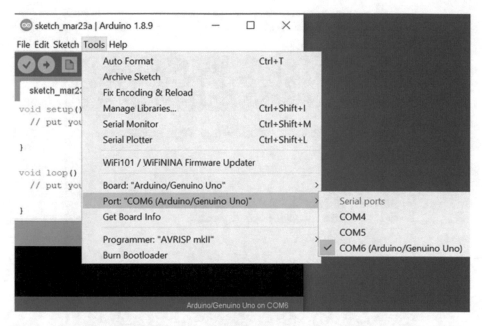

Figure 3-4. *Connection to the Arduino can be confirmed by checking the Port connection*

Running a First Sketch

Figure 3-5 shows a short program to introduce ideas in programming the Arduino with IDE. A line of code has been put into the setup section with the command:

```
Serial.begin(9600);    //Start serial communication
```

Figure 3-5. *A sketch for printing over a serial connection*

Since this command is the setup section, it runs only once, serving here to initialize communication between the Arduino and the host computer. The 9600 indicates a baud rate, a speed at which communication takes place. The end of a command is indicated with a semicolon. The // indicates the start of a comment, which continues to the end of the current line.

The loop section runs over and over again, in this case printing "Hello!" every second over a serial communication link. Two commands accomplish this:

```
Serial.println("Hello!");    //Print to serial
delay(1000);    //Pause for 1 second
```

Just as in the setup section, commands in the loop section end with a semicolon. The numeral in the delay command is in milliseconds, creating a pause in this example of 1 second.

Once the program commands have been written, the sketch can be uploaded and executed by clicking the Upload icon (an arrow pointing right) on the toolbar. The results of this program can be viewed by going to the toolbar in the IDE to select Tools ➤ Serial Monitor, as shown in Figure 3-6. The word "Hello!" is printed every 1 second. An important feature in the Serial Monitor is the baud setting, which has to match the baud rate set in the sketch, 9600 in this case.

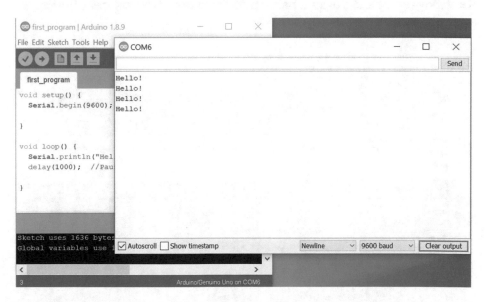

Figure 3-6. *Opening the Serial Monitor should show "Hello!" printed every 1 second*

More sophisticated programs will be used in the upcoming chapters of this book, adapted from various websites to be run in the IDE. A sketch can be copied from a website and then pasted inside the IDE. The Serial Monitor will be used in several of the projects of this book as a diagnostic, showing sensor readings as a check for proper operation.

Working with Libraries

Many sensors and devices that connect to the Arduino have sets of commands written for them in the form of a Library. Arduino sketches often make use of these Libraries to work with external devices, calling up advanced functions with simple commands. Libraries can be found in the IDE by going to the toolbar to select Tools ➤ Manage Libraries, which brings up the screen shown in Figure 3-7. A particular Library of interest has to be installed into the IDE by clicking the Install link that appears in the Library listing. The Library for a particular sensor or device can be found by typing the device's name into the search window near the top of the Library Manager.

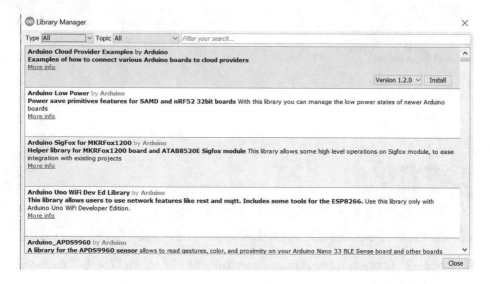

Figure 3-7. *Libraries are installed from the Library Manager*

Once the Library is installed in the IDE, the Library gets called into the sketch by the command # include, such as in Figure 3-8, where the Library is being called that controls the Qwiic LED Stick used in Chapter 6. The # include command goes before the setup section of a sketch.

A Library can be accessed in various places in a sketch to program sensor or device functions with a single line of code. Example commands, taking the Qwiic LED Stick of Chapter 6 as an example, are LEDStick.begin() or LEDStick.LEDoff().

The details on how Libraries work or how to call subroutines aren't critical to understand for the projects in this book. These details are handled within the sketches available for use from sensor manufacturers and experienced users. However, as described in this section, the Libraries need to be installed into the Arduino IDE for these copy-pasted sketches to function.

Figure 3-8. *A Library gets called into a sketch by the # include command*

Working with Functions

A function in an Arduino sketch is a subroutine often used when a section of code is needed several times. It is analogous to a My Block in EV3 code. Using a function can cut down on program complexity if the same code is used repeatedly in a sketch. Figure 3-9 shows a sketch that adds two numbers. The two numbers to add are first defined at the beginning of the sketch, using int to declare these numbers as variables. The function, called simpleAddFunction in this example, is written at the bottom of the sketch, after the loop section of code. And in the loop itself, the function is called, with the values x and y passed to the function to return the sum. The variables defined in the function are called a and b as a placeholder for values that will be passed by the main section of the sketch—x and y are the values passed to the function in this example. This simple example, meant to show the structure and use of a function, isn't really necessary for such a simple operation. However, as will be seen in the examples of this book, a function may be called multiple times, simplifying the sketch. Some projects make use of multiple functions, with each of the functions appearing after the sketch's loop.

```
function_program                                              ▼

int x = 2;   //Define variable as integer and assign value   ∧
int y = 3;   //Define variable as integer and assign value
int k;    //Define variable


void setup() {
  Serial.begin(9600);   //Start serial communication

}

void loop() {
  k = simpleAddFunction(x, y);     //Call function
  Serial.println(k);   //Print to serial
  delay(1000);   //Pause for 1 second

}

int simpleAddFunction(int a, int b) {    //Define function
  int sum;    //Define variable as integer
  sum = a + b;  //Math operation
  return sum;    //Return value to loop
}
                                                              ∨
```

Figure 3-9. *The function, named simpleAddFunction in this example, appears at the bottom of the sketch*

Summary

This chapter gave a quick-start guide to programming the Arduino via the Integrated Development Environment (IDE). The IDE is installed on a host computer for connection to the Arduino Uno by a USB cable. Arduino programs are called sketches, featuring two main parts: a setup for executing commands once and a loop for infinite repetition of commands. If the program uses variables, they are declared before the setup section. A simple program was presented to demonstrate a connection to an Arduino. Building sophisticated programs is not described in this book, using instead sketches developed by sensor and device manufacturers that can be copied and pasted into the IDE. These premade sketches often involve the use of Libraries, so a primer was given on how to find and install a Library for a particular device. Sketches also often make use of functions for efficient programs, so an introduction was also given on functions.

CHAPTER 4

Sensors and Electronics

A guide is presented in this chapter on finding and selecting various sensors to match with an Arduino. An overview is first given of LEGO-based devices, just to make sure that a MINDSTORMS-ready device is already not available for a desired function. Also, LEGO sensors and Arduino sensors can be combined in a project, as is done in all the projects in this book. Arduino-based sensors offer many complex and interesting applications, so guidance is then given on finding and selecting these devices. Communications interfaces are an important aspect of using Arduino sensors, so sensors are classified in this chapter by their interface. Some designs require electronic circuits for use, typically involving resistors and capacitors, so an introduction is given on these electronic components.

MINDSTORMS Sensors and Motors

The easiest devices to use for MINDSTORMS inventions are, of course, the sensors and motors built by LEGO. Table 4-1 summarizes these devices. The MINDSTORMS EV3 31313 set comes with some of the sensors made by LEGO including the Infrared Sensor, Color Sensor, and Touch Sensor. The other sensors available can be purchased separately. It's noteworthy that EV3 motors are dual use, in providing sensing of rotation angle in addition to their motor function.

© Grady Koch 2020
G. Koch, *The LEGO Arduino Cookbook*, https://doi.org/10.1007/978-1-4842-6303-7_4

Table 4-1. *Summary of LEGO-made sensors and motors*

Device	Part Number	Function
Large Motor	95658	Servo, also rotation angle sensor
Medium Motor	99455	Servo, also rotation angle sensor
Infrared Sensor	95654	Proximity, beacon, remote control receiver
Touch Sensor	95648	Pressing, bumping
Color Sensor	95650	Color, ambient light, reflected light intensity
Gyro Sensor	99380	Rotation angle, rotation rate
Ultrasonic Sensor	95652	Distance, presence of another ultrasonic transmitter
Temperature Sensor	9749	Temperature

Aftermarket MINDSTORMS-Compatible Sensors

LEGO-made MINDSTORMS sensors are somewhat simple in nature, intended for the application of small robots and vehicles. To build more sophisticated projects, several companies have developed MINDSTORMS-compatible sensors and controllers. Ease of use is allowed by downloadable software programming blocks and LEGO-compatible mounting holes. Aftermarket suppliers include

- Mindsensors.com

- Dexter Industries (`www.dexterindustries.com`)

- Vernier (`www.vernier.com`)

An example of aftermarket sensors is shown in Figure 4-1 of a programmable LED matrix and a camera, both from Mindsensors.com. Both of these devices will be used in projects in later chapters.

Figure 4-1. *Two example aftermarket MINDSTORMS-compatible sensors include a camera (at the left) and an LED matrix (at the right)*

Arduino Sensors

The lure of Arduino sensors is a vast variety of applications, well beyond the capability of ready-made MINDSTORMS sensors. These sensors are usually available with Arduino programming sketches made by the sensor's manufacturer or distributor. Such distributors include

- SparkFun (www.sparkfun.com)

- Seeed (www.seeedstudio.com)

- DFROBOT (www.dfrobot.com)

- Adafruit (www.adafruit.com)

Sensors communicate with the Arduino in various ways, such as pulse-width modulation (PWM), inter-integrated circuit (I2C), and serial peripheral interface (SPI). Each of these communication protocols involves complex designs on clock speeds, voltage levels, device addressing, and digital representation of numbers. However, knowledge of such details is not needed to use the sensor device since the Arduino and associated programming sketches handle this complexity.

Sometimes communication interfaces interfere with each other when working with multiple devices or across host devices, such as between the Arduino and EV3 Intelligent Brick. For example, I2C communication will be used in some projects of this book to transfer data from the Arduino to the EV3 Intelligent Brick. In this situation, the use of an I2C-based sensor becomes problematic, and a different type of sensor interface should be used. Details on the different types of sensor interfaces are given in the following sections.

Pulse-Width Modulation (PWM)

Pulse-width modulation (PWM) is a simple way to encode information and is an output format on both the Arduino and the EV3 Intelligent Brick. Information is encoded by changing the length of time that a digital logic signal is high within a certain time span, usually represented by a 5-volt signal. Figure 4-2 diagrams several levels of PWM with levels of modulation described as a percentage. For example, 0 modulation is indicated by the signal being completely off, 25% has the signal level on for ¼ of the time, and 50% for ½ the time. The duration of the timing is the time between rising edges of adjacent pulses, which is referred to as the *period*. Signals are commonly characterized by the inverse of the time period, which is called *frequency*. Sensors with a PWM output use the amount of modulation to describe some quantity of interest.

For example, Chapter 8 will work with a lidar sensor that indicates measured distance as being proportional to the amount of modulation. PWM will also come into play in Chapters 5 and 6 as outputs from the Arduino and EV3 Intelligent Brick.

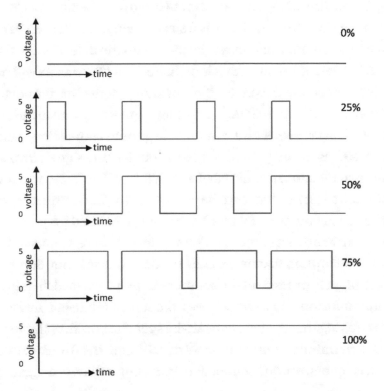

Figure 4-2. *Pulse-width modulation (PWM) involves turning on a signal for a fraction of a time span*

Inter-integrated Circuit (I2C) Interface

The inter-integrated circuit (I2C) format is commonly used to pass bytes of data between electronic devices. These bytes of data can consist of a number that indicates a quantity being measured or the status of a sensor. I2C consists of signals sent over two wire connections: a clock line and a data line. The clock line is a steady frequency that serves as a reference to when information will be passed on the data line; the data line contains the information that is of interest. So I2C sensors will have one solder connection or wire for the clock and another for the data, often abbreviated as "SCL" and "SDA." Two other connections are involved with an I2C sensor: power and ground. The ground connection, usually labeled "GND," is the 0V (0-volt) reference for all of the signals involved. The power connection, usually labeled "PWR," "5V," or "3.3V," can involve some complication in what it's to be connected to. The Arduino board offers two voltage outputs (5V and 3.3V) that can be used for power, which are important to not get confused. The sensor should be connected to the Arduino power option that matches its needed voltage input. Sometimes, the power input is printed on the sensor's circuit board, which helps to eliminate confusion. But in some cases, the sensor is labeled only with "PWR," requiring that the user consult the specification sheet for the sensor to determine whether to use 5V or 3.3V from the Arduino. In the following chapters, the I2C connection, including power, is diagrammed to avoid confusion.

Serial Peripheral Interface (SPI)

Another common sensor interface is the serial peripheral interface (SPI). SPI is a little more sophisticated in allowing data to both transmit and receive at the same time, whereas I2C can only transmit or receive at one time. This higher level of capability for SPI involves two more wire connections than I2C, for a total of six connections for an SPI interface. There is often much variation among sensor manufacturers in how SPI connections are labeled, but a frequently encountered labeling format is

- SDO: Serial data output

- CS: Chip select—selects which device of a pair is transmitting and which is receiving

- SCK: Serial clock signal

- SDI: Serial data input

- 3V3: Power connection to 3.3V

- GND: Ground connection

An example SPI sensor is used in Chapter 9, with diagrams and explanation of how the sensor is connected to the Arduino.

Electronic Components

Some sensors have the user add electronic components to select a particular function of a sensor or to shift the voltage levels of signals. Such level shifting, typically accomplished with a *resistor*, is sometimes required to make a signal compatible with the input of another electronic device being used. A resistor, shown in physical appearance in Figure 4-3 and in schematic representation in Figure 4-4, is a device that converts electrical energy into heat. Also, some occasions require converting PWM signals to analog signals, which can be done with a combination of a resistor and a capacitor. A *capacitor*, also shown in Figures 4-3 and 4-4, is a device that stores electrical energy. Details on identifying the specifics of resistors and capacitors are given in the following.

Figure 4-3. *A resistor (at the left) has colored rings that identify its resistance value, 4700 ohms in this case. A capacitor (at the right) has a numeric label to indicate its capacitance value, 1 μF in this example*

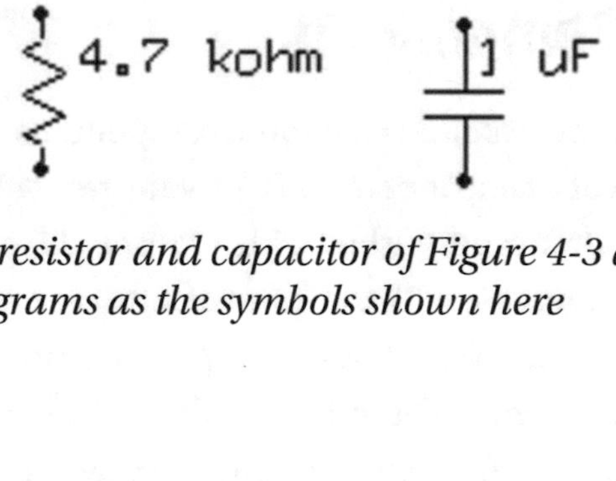

Figure 4-4. *The resistor and capacitor of Figure 4-3 are represented in schematic diagrams as the symbols shown here*

Resistors

Resistors limit the flow of current as per *Ohm's Law*:

$$i = \frac{V}{R}$$

where i is the current, V is the voltage, and R is the resistance value of the resistor. Hence, larger values of resistance will give a lower current through the resistor. The value of a resistor is indicated by colored bands around the resistor, as per Table 4-2. For example, the resistor in Figure 4-3 has bands colored yellow, which indicates the first digit of the resistance value is 4; violet, indicating the second digit is 7; red, which means the power of 10 multiplier is 2; and gold representing a tolerance of ±5%. Thus, this is a 4700-ohm resistor (47×10^2) of 5% tolerance.

Table 4-2. *Resistance values can be read from the colored rings printed on the resistor*

Color	First Band (First Digit)	Second Band (Second Digit)	Third Band (Multiplier)	Fourth Band (Tolerance)
Black	0	0	1 Ω	± 1%
Brown	1	1	10 Ω	± 2%
Red	2	2	100 Ω	
Orange	3	3	1 kΩ	
Yellow	4	4	10 kΩ	
Green	5	5	100 kΩ	± 0.5%
Blue	6	6	1 MΩ	± 0.25%
Violet	7	7	10 MΩ	± 0.10%
Gray	8	8	100 MΩ	± 0.05%
White	9	9	1 GΩ	
Gold				± 5%
Silver				± 10%

Tolerance is an indication of how well the actual resistance compares to the intended value, since the manufacturing process introduces some error. For example, the 5% tolerance of the 4700-Ω resistor of Figure 4-4 means that the actual resistance could be anywhere from 4465 Ω to 4935 Ω. This range of values is good enough for all the projects in this book. Some applications require the resistor to be more exact, so there are resistors available with very low tolerances. But better tolerances come at the expense of cost, and there's no need for the purposes of this book to buy better than the commonly available 5% tolerance.

Another specification for a resistor is in how much power it can handle. Since resistors convert electrical energy into heat, it's possible for a resistor to get so hot that it will burn up. Resistors are made to handle specific levels of power load, with higher power resistors costing more and having physically larger size. To determine the power going through a resistor, the power can be calculated by

$$P = V \times i$$

where P is the power, V is the voltage across the resistor in volts, and i is the current through the resistor in amps. The resulting calculation will have units of watts. For the uses in this book, the power involved is rather low, matching the commonly available resistor power handling capability of 1/4 watt.

Resistors can be purchased at many online stores, including `www.amazon.com`, `www.sparkfun.com`, `www.digikey.com`, `www.mouser.com`, and `www.adafruit.com`. Many of these online stores also sell the Arduino sensors that are found in later chapters, so resistors can be bought on the same order as an Arduino or a sensor. Resistors are inexpensive, so it's a convenient arrangement to buy a kit of resistors to have a range of resistances to pick from. The online stores mentioned earlier offer such kits of ¼ watt resistors.

Capacitors

Capacitors store electrical charge to discharge as needed. The function of a capacitor can be described by the equation

$$i = C\frac{dV}{dt}$$

where i is the current through the capacitor, C is the capacitance value of the capacitor, and dV/dt is the derivative, or rate of change, of voltage with respect to time. This equation shows a key feature of the capacitor in that it only allows current flow when the applied voltage is changing. So, if the applied voltage is constant, there is no current flow through a capacitor. Capacitance is quantified in units of farads, with typical values being quite small, on the order of millionths of a farad, abbreviated as microfarads or µF. The value of a capacitor is labeled on the device in three digits, with the first two digits being the first two digits of the capacitance value. The third digit is an exponent of 10, forming a multiplier for the first two digits. For example, the capacitor in Figure 4-3 is labeled "105," meaning

$$10 \times 10^5 = 10^6$$

This number represents the capacitance in picofarads (10^{12} farads). Reducing the exponents further gives

$$10^6 \times 10^{-12} = 10^{-6} \text{ farads} = 1\mu F$$

Hence, the capacitor in Figure 4-3 has a capacitance of 1 µF.

Capacitors can be purchased at the online electronics stores mentioned earlier for buying resistors. Kits are also an option to buy a variety of capacitances for other electronic projects that come up, but only one type of capacitor is used in the projects of this book—a 1-µF ceramic capacitor.

Summary

Arduino sensors offer many new opportunities for MINDSTORMS inventions, as described in later chapters. However, if a LEGO-made sensor can offer the needed functionality, then the implementation is best made with a LEGO sensor. Many projects use multiple sensors or motors, and so Arduino and LEGO-made devices can be combined. Many non-LEGO sensor options also exist that are compatible with MINDSTORMS, including downloadable programming blocks, offering another option for ease of use. As will be seen in the projects of this book, combinations are made of Arduino, LEGO, and non-LEGO MINDSTORMS-compatible sensors. Arduino sensors can be classified by how the sensor communicates with the Arduino, so an introduction was given on the common types of interfaces including pulse-width modulation (PWM), inter-integrated circuit (I2C), and serial peripheral interface (SPI). Sensor implementation sometimes requires the use of resistor or capacitor electronic devices, so an overview was given of how these components work and how to find them for purchase.

CHAPTER 5

The LEGO Metal Detector—I2C Sensor with EV3 Analog Interface

This chapter examines analog output from the Arduino to be read by the EV3 Intelligent Brick. An example application will be presented of building a metal detector, based on the Grove Inductive Sensor, shown in Figure 5-1. This sensor detects the presence of metal by creating a magnetic field. When a metal is within this magnetic field, an electrical current is induced in the metal, changing the magnetic field created by the sensor. This change in magnetic field is quantified by the Grove Inductive Sensor to give an indication of a nearby presence of a metal. The control of the Grove Inductive Sensor is by an Arduino sketch, which also creates a pulse-width modulation output related to the sensor's measurement. This pulse-width modulation signal is converted to an analog signal by a low-pass filter, thereby creating an analog signal that can be read by the EV3 Intelligent Brick.

© Grady Koch 2020
G. Koch, *The LEGO Arduino Cookbook*, https://doi.org/10.1007/978-1-4842-6303-7_5

Figure 5-1. *The coil on the right side of the Grove Inductive Sensor creates a magnetic field to detect the presence of a nearby metal*

Mounting the Grove Inductive Sensor

The Grove Inductive Sensor is part of the Grove line of devices made by Seeed (`www.seeedstudio.com`). This product line also includes an adapter to hold Grove devices with LEGO-compatible mounting holes. The Inductive Sensor mounted in one of these Grove Wrappers is shown in Figure 5-2. With this convenient mounting of the sensor, it can be attached to the LEGO Arduino Workstation, as shown in Figure 5-3.

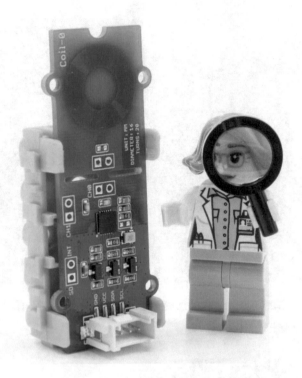

Figure 5-2. *A Grove Wrapper serves to hold the Grove Inductive Sensor and provide LEGO mounting*

Figure 5-3. *The Grove Wrapper can be pressed onto the LEGO Arduino Workstation*

The Low-Pass Filter

The Arduino has no way to output an analog voltage. But it can produce a pulse-width modulation output that can be converted to an analog voltage with a low-pass filter. This filter passes low frequencies from an input signal, but blocks high frequencies. A low-pass filter can be built from a resistor and capacitor, called an *RC circuit*, illustrated in Figure 5-4. The way an RC circuit acts as a filter can be understood by noting that the reactance of a capacitor depends on frequency in a relationship quantified as

$$X_c = \frac{1}{2\pi fC}$$

where X_c is the reactance of the capacitor, f is the frequency of the input signal, and C is the capacitance. *Reactance* is similar to resistance, except that reactance varies with frequency. For low values of frequency, the reactance is very high for the capacitor. Low-frequency inputs do not flow well through the capacitor, so the output voltage in the circuit of Figure 5-4 keeps all the low-frequency components of the input voltage. But for high frequencies, the reactance of the capacitor is quite low, so all the high-frequency inputs to the circuit get shorted to ground. The output voltage then is just the low-frequency components of the input voltage.

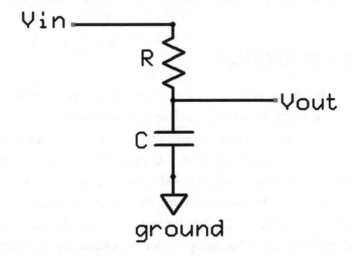

Figure 5-4. *A low-pass filter can be implemented with an RC circuit*

The question to consider then in designing the RC low-pass filter is of what is considered to be a low frequency and what is considered to be a high frequency. High and low frequencies can be quantified as being below or above a design parameter known as *cutoff frequency*. The cutoff frequency can be calculated as

$$f_c = \frac{1}{2\pi RC}$$

where f_c is the cutoff frequency, R is the resistor value, and C is the capacitor value. For a 4.7-kΩ resistor and 1-μF capacitor, as will be used in the design here, the cutoff frequency is 33.9 Hz. So frequencies above

33.9 Hz will start to be blocked. If the pulse-width modulation input is at a frequency much higher than this cutoff frequency, then the low-pass filter output will be a DC analog voltage. As will be implemented in a sketch in a later section, the Arduino will be set up to have a pulse-width modulation frequency of 63 kHz, more than 1000 times higher than the cutoff frequency and certain to result in a smooth DC analog voltage. Implementing the low-pass filter is described in the following section.

Wiring Connections

Three sets of wiring connections are needed: (1) the Grove Inductive Sensor to Arduino, (2) the Arduino to Breadboard Connector, and (3) the Breadboard Connector to EV3 Intelligent Brick. The Grove Inductive Sensor to Arduino connection is shown in Figure 5-5 using the cable supplied with sensor. One end of this cable needs to have its connector cut off and wires stripped to expose wires that can be plugged into the breadboard. The wires from this cable are stranded, so they should be tinned with solder to make them rigid. *Tinning* a stranded wire involves melting solder onto the strands of the wire so that all the strands are fused together. Another option is to purchase the Grove cable (4-pin Male Jumper to Grove 4-pin Conversion Cable) from Seeed (`www.seeedstudio.com`) that has jumper wire connections on one end.

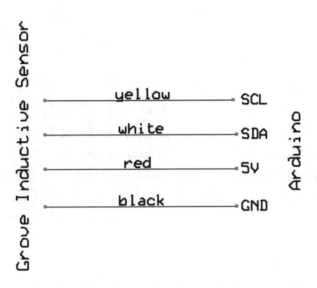

Figure 5-5. *Connection between the Grove Inductive Sensor and the Arduino is by a four-wire cable*

The second set of wire connections links the Arduino to the EV3 Intelligent Brick via the Breadboard Connector Adapter. These connections are diagrammed in Figure 5-6. These connections include the low-pass filter based on a 4.7-kΩ resistor and 1-µF capacitor. The output from this RC filter is read into the EV3 Intelligent Brick on the AN IN pin connection.

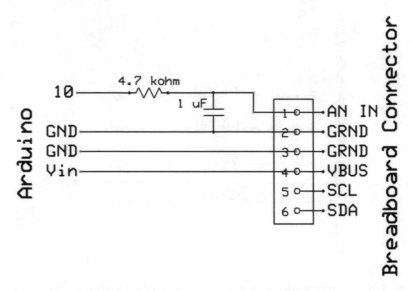

Figure 5-6. *Connection between the Arduino and the breadboard includes an RC circuit to convert the pulse-width modulation on the Arduino pin 10 to a DC voltage*

A third connection is an EV3 Connector Cable between the EV3 Intelligent Brick port 4 and the Breadboard Connector, as diagrammed in Figure 5-7.

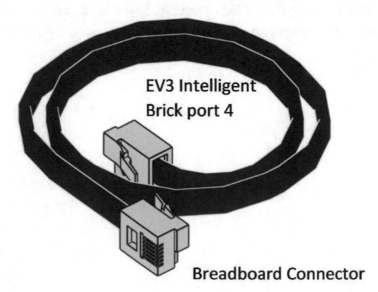

Figure 5-7. *Connection of the EV3 Intelligent Brick is by port 4*

EV3 Code

The EV3 program, shown in Figure 5-8, reads the analog voltage created by the filtered Arduino output. A Raw Sensor Value block is used to read the analog voltage on port 4. A series of tests is then performed to determine if the voltage being read is within a certain range, corresponding to metal being detected within a certain distance of the Grove Inductive Sensor. Light and sounds on the EV3 Intelligent Brick give an indication of the detection and distance away from metal.

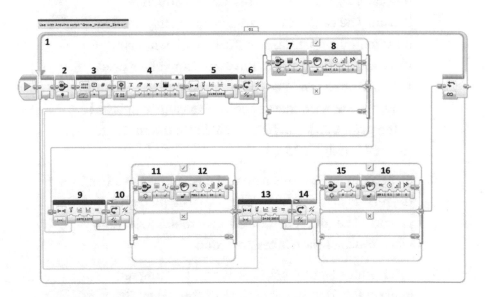

Figure 5-8. *The EV3 code for the LEGO Metal Detector reads an analog signal by a Raw Sensor Value block*

Steps in the program include

1. Loop Block: Sets up an infinite repetition of measuring input voltage and checking for detection of metal.

2. Brick Status Light Block: Turns off the front panel light of the EV3 Intelligent Brick, clearing out any prior indication of metal detection.

3. Raw Sensor Value Block: Reads the voltage on the AN IN pin of port 4. Voltages are converted to a unitless measurement of 0 to 4095. A reading of 4095 corresponds to an input of 5V.

4. Display Block: Indicates the value read in the prior block on the front panel of the EV3 Intelligent Brick.

5. Range Block: Tests for a measured signal between values of 1150 to 1450, which indicates a metal object being very close to the Grove Inductive Sensor. The values to use in this range may need to be adjusted, depending on the type of metal and variations in the resistor and capacitor values used to build the RC low-pass filter. The metal used in this example was a US quarter coin. The value displayed in the prior block can help to calibrate the values to use in the range settings.

6. Switch Block: Presents true and false paths based on the results of the Range block. The true path gives an audible and visual indication of metal detection, while the false path takes no action.

7. Brick Status Light Block: Turns on a flashing red light on the front panel of the EV3 Intelligent Brick to start the true path of the Switch block.

8. Sound Block: Activates a beeping sound on the EV3 Intelligent Brick's speaker. This sound accompanies the blinking red light turned on in the previous block.

9-12.   Repeat the signal test as done in blocks 5–8, but for a metal located a little farther away than the case for blocks 5–8. To distinguish that the detected metal is farther away, the indication on the EV3 Intelligent Brick is a yellow light and lower-frequency tone.

13–16.   Repeat the signal test as done in blocks 9–12, but for a metal located a little farther away than the case for blocks 9–12. To distinguish that the detected metal is farther away, the indication on the EV3 Intelligent Brick is a green light and lower-frequency tone.

Arduino Sketch

The Arduino sketch for running the Grove Inductive Sensor is shown in Listing 5-1, largely based on the coin_test_demo.ino example script on the www.github.com/Seeed-Studio site. A library is needed to run the Grove Inductive Sensor, called Seeed_LDC1612.h, also available on the GitHub site.

Listing 5-1. The Arduino sketch for using the Grove Inductive Sensor should be run at the same time as the EV3 program "metal_detector".

```
/*------------------------------------------------------
Grove Inductive Sensor
Takes measurements from the Grove LDC1612 Inductive Sensor to
detect the presence of metal.
The test case of metal was a US quarter coin.
If a metal is detected, this sketch sends a signal on Arduino
Pin 10 with pulse-width modulation
related to how far away the coin is located.
```

Connections:
Grove 5-V (red) to Arduino 5V
Grove Ground (black) to Arduino GND
Grove SCL (yellow) to Arduino SCL
Grove SDA (white) to Arduino SDA
Arduino pin 10 to RC filter (4.7kohm & 1uF) to Breadboard
Connector AN IN
EV3 Breadboard Connector VBUS to Arduino VIN
EV3 Breadboard Connector GND (both of them) to Arduino GND
EV3 cable between Breadboard Connector and Port 4 on EV3
Intelligent Brick

Run program on EV3 Intelligent Brick called "metal_detector".

This sketch was modified from github.com/Seeed-Studio/Seeed_
LDC1612/blob/master/examples/coin_test_demo

---*/

#include "Seeed_LDC1612.h" //Call library for LDC Inductive
Sensor

LDC1612 sensor;

//Define constants for various detection ranges.
const u32 DISTANCE_00_01=60000000;   // distance:<1mm
const u32 DISTANCE_01_05=45000000;   // distance:1mm~5mm
const u32 DISTANCE_05_10=44250000;   // distance:5mm~10mm
const u32 DISTANCE_10_15=44080000;   // distance:10mm~15mm
const u32 DISTANCE_15_20=44020000;   // distance:15mm~20mm

void setup()

{

```
Serial.begin(9600); //Start serial communications.  Serial
monitor must match this baud rate.
delay(100);
Serial.println("start!");

sensor.init();

if(sensor.single_channel_config(CHANNEL_0))
//Check for error with Grove device connection.

{
    Serial.println("can't detect sensor!");
    while(1);
}

}

void loop()

{

    u32 result_channel1=0;
    setPwmFrequency(10,1);  //Set frequency of PWM higher than
                            default

    /*Get channel 0 result and parse it.*/

    sensor.get_channel_result(CHANNEL_0,&result_channel1);

        if(result_channel1>=DISTANCE_00_01)

        {
            Serial.println("The distance to metal is 0~1mm");
            analogWrite(10, 0); //Set pin 10 for 0/255 PWM
        }
```

```
        if(result_channel1<DISTANCE_00_01&&result_
        channel1>=DISTANCE_01_05)

        {
            Serial.println("The distance to metal is 1~5mm");
            analogWrite(10, 75);  //Set pin 10 for 75/255 PWM
        }

        if(result_channel1<DISTANCE_01_05&&result_
        channel1>=DISTANCE_05_10)

        {
            Serial.println("The distance to metal is 5~10mm");
            analogWrite(10, 150);  //Set pin 10 for 150/255 PWM
        }

        if(result_channel1<DISTANCE_05_10&&result_
        channel1>=DISTANCE_10_15)

        {
            Serial.println("No metal detected.");
            analogWrite(10, 200);  //Set pin 10 for 200/255 PWM
        }

        delay(1000);
}

//Function for raising pulsewidth modulation frequency

void setPwmFrequency(int pin, int divisor) {
  byte mode;
  if(pin == 5 || pin == 6 || pin == 9 || pin == 10) {
    switch(divisor) {
      case 1: mode = 0x01; break;
```

```
      case 8: mode = 0x02; break;
      case 64: mode = 0x03; break;
      case 256: mode = 0x04; break;
      case 1024: mode = 0x05; break;
      default: return;
    }
    if(pin == 5 || pin == 6) {
      TCCR0B = TCCR0B & 0b11111000 | mode;
    } else {
      TCCR1B = TCCR1B & 0b11111000 | mode;
    }
  } else if(pin == 3 || pin == 11) {
    switch(divisor) {
      case 1: mode = 0x01; break;
      case 8: mode = 0x02; break;
      case 32: mode = 0x03; break;
      case 64: mode = 0x04; break;
      case 128: mode = 0x05; break;
      case 256: mode = 0x06; break;
      case 1024: mode = 0x07; break;
      default: return;
    }
    TCCR2B = TCCR2B & 0b11111000 | mode;
  }
}
```

Results

The EV3 program indicates four possible conditions: nothing detected, metal within 0–1 mm, metal within 1–5 mm, and metal within 5–10 mm. A video of the operation can be seen on www.hightechlego.com. Each of these conditions is assigned a different level of pulse-width modulation on the Arduino pin 10. Figure 5-9 shows the unfiltered output as viewed by an oscilloscope on pin 10 for the four conditions. After passing through the RC low-pass filter, the DC voltages of Figure 5-10 result.

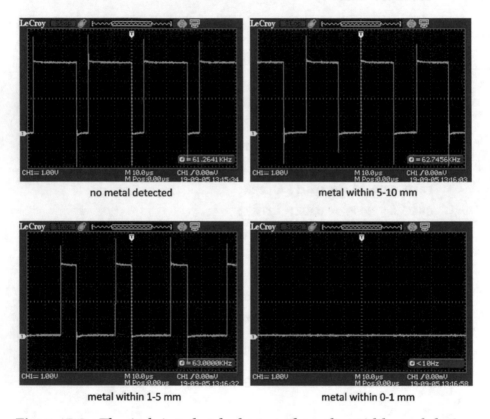

Figure 5-9. *The Arduino sketch changes the pulse-width modulation output on pin 10 as metal is detected at various distances*

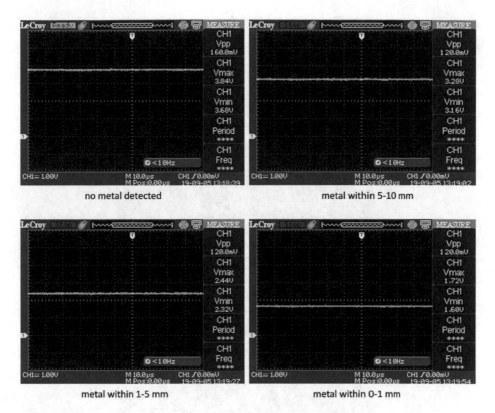

Figure 5-10. The RC filter output is a DC voltage of level corresponding to the length of pulse-width modulation

Alternate Mount

The LEGO Arduino Workstation is useful for developing and testing the LEGO metal detector, but a more compact handheld version could have advantages. Such a handheld implementation is shown in Figure 5-11, useful for searching people for hidden metal objects. Building instructions follow Figure 5-11.

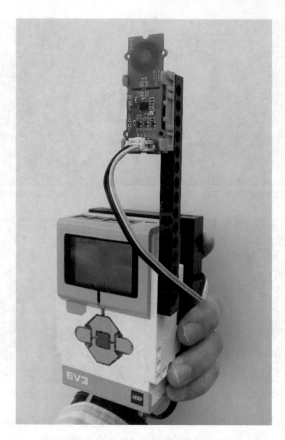

Figure 5-11.   *The STEMTera can be attached to the back of the EV3 Intelligent Brick for a handheld metal detector*

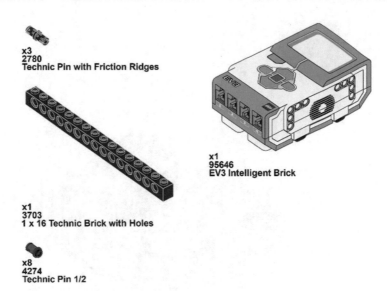

x3
2780
Technic Pin with Friction Ridges

x1
95646
EV3 Intelligent Brick

x1
3703
1 x 16 Technic Brick with Holes

x8
4274
Technic Pin 1/2

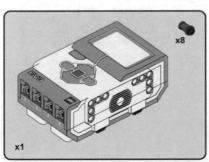

x8

x1

1

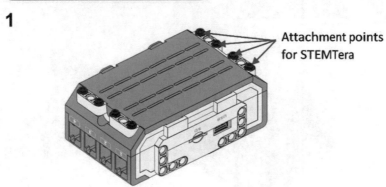

Attachment points
for STEMTera

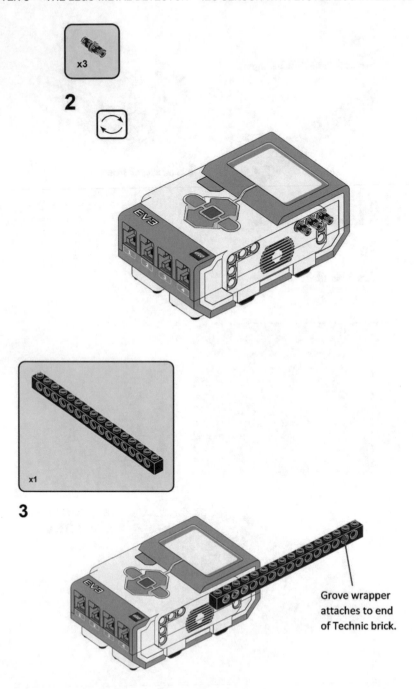

Grove wrapper attaches to end of Technic brick.

Summary

In this chapter, a technique was developed for passing analog voltages from the Arduino to the EV3 Intelligent Brick. The Arduino does not have an output specifically for creating an analog signal. However, the Arduino's pulse-width modulation output can be converted to an analog signal by the use of a low-pass filter. Such a filter was built from a simple RC circuit. An example application was demonstrated, building a metal detector based on a Grove Inductive Sensor. This sensor measurement of the presence of metals was translated into an analog voltage that can be used by the EV3 Intelligent Brick to indicate the presence of and distance to a metal object. In the next chapter, the analog voltage interface will be considered going in the opposite direction, from the EV3 Intelligent Brick to the Arduino.

CHAPTER 6

Programmable LEDs—I2C Controller with EV3 Analog Interface

This chapter continues working with analog signals, sending voltages from the EV3 Intelligent Brick to the Arduino. The previous chapter had signals going from the Arduino to the EV3; in this chapter, the reverse is being done. An example application is developed of the EV3 Intelligent Brick sending commands to select different patterns on an LED array. This LED array, shown in Figure 6-1, is a line of ten LEDs that can be programmed by the Arduino to light up each LED in color and brightness. Three buttons on the EV3 Intelligent Brick will select which of the three color patterns will be played.

© Grady Koch 2020
G. Koch, *The LEGO Arduino Cookbook*, https://doi.org/10.1007/978-1-4842-6303-7_6

Figure 6-1. *The Qwiic LED Stick is a linear array of programmable LEDs*

Mounting the Qwiic LED Stick

The LED array is implemented with the Qwiic LED Stick, available at
www.sparkfun.com. Example Arduino sketches are available at https://
github.com/sparkfun/SparkFun_Qwiic_LED_Stick_Arduino_Library to
set various display patterns on the array or to program custom displays.
The Qwiic LED Stick has mounting holes at the corners of its printed
circuit board that line up with LEGO spacing, so it can be attached to a
Technic brick, as has been done in Figure 6-2. This configuration can then
be attached to the LEGO Arduino Workstation, pictured in Figure 6-3.

Figure 6-2. *The mounting holes on the circuit board of the Qwiic LED Stick line up with holes of a 1 × 14 Technic Brick with Holes, through which M3 machine screws can be inserted*

Figure 6-3. *The mounted Qwiic LED Stick can be attached to the LEGO Arduino Workstation*

Wiring Connections

Three sets of wire connections are needed: (1) the Qwiic LED Stick to Arduino (2) the Arduino to Breadboard Connector, and (3) the Breadboard Connector to EV3 Intelligent Brick. The Qwiic LED Stick to Arduino connection is shown in Figure 6-4, easily implemented with a cable made by SparkFun (`www.sparkfun.com`) called Qwiic Cable-Breadboard Jumper seen in the photograph of Figure 6-3. This Qwiic cable has four colored wires, connected as shown in Figure 6-4. Care is needed to connect the red power cable to 3.3V on the Arduino, not the 5V source.

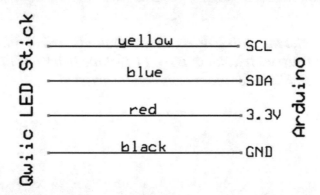

Figure 6-4. *Connection between the Qwiic LED Stick and the Arduino is by a four-wire cable*

The second set of wire connections links the Arduino to the EV3 Intelligent Brick via a Breadboard Connector. The connection to make is diagrammed in Figure 6-5. A 1-kΩ and 10-kΩ resistor circuit is needed in this setup to replace the feedback signals associated with controlling this connection with an Unregulated Motor block. In other words, the voltages coming from this resistor circuit convince the EV3 Intelligent Brick that the connection is to a motor. Another simple circuit, of a 1-µF capacitor and 4.7-kohm resistor, is connected to AN IN to convert the pulse-width modulation output from AN IN to a DC voltage. This conversion is described in the following section.

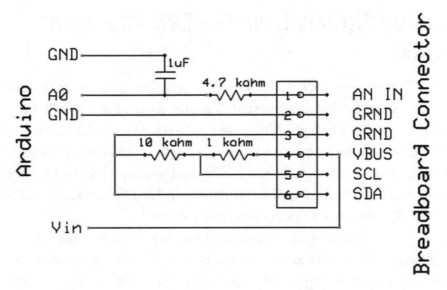

Figure 6-5. *Connection from the breakout board involves a few electronic components*

A third connection is by an EV3 Connector Cable between the EV3 Intelligent Brick port 4 and the Breadboard Connector, as diagrammed in Figure 6-6.

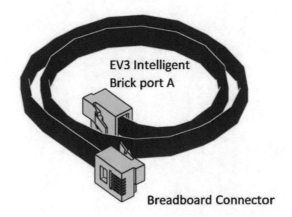

Figure 6-6. *Connection of the EV3 Intelligent Brick is to port A*

Analog Signals from the EV3 Intelligent Brick

The EV3 Intelligent Brick does not have a capability to provide a DC analog output, just as the Arduino does not. But, also, as was the case with the Arduino, the EV3 Intelligent Brick can produce a pulse-width modulation output that can be converted with an RC circuit to a DC analog voltage. The RC circuit design is the same as that used in Chapter 5, involving a 4.7-kohm resistor in a series with a 1-μF capacitor. The implementation of this RC circuit is shown in the schematic of Figure 6-5.

The control of the pulse-width modulation output from the EV3 Intelligent Brick can be accomplished by using the Unregulated Motor block. The input setting on this block is for power with a range of −100 to 100%. To create a positive voltage from the wiring connection of Figure 6-5, only the positive range of values should be used. The variation of the pulse-width modulation output for various power settings on the Unregulated Motor block is shown in Figure 6-7.

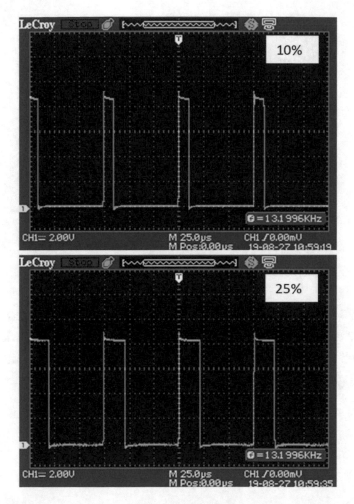

Figure 6-7. *An oscilloscope connected to the AN IN pin on the Breadboard Connector shows a pulse-width modulation signal at 13.2 kHz frequency—the depth of modulation changes with power setting on the Unregulated Motor block*

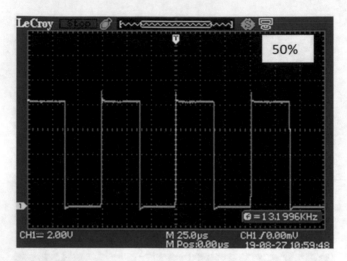

Figure 6-7. *(continued)*

An EV3 program for selecting the three different pulse widths of Figure 6-7 is shown in Figure 6-8. With this program, the pulse width can be selected by hitting the left, right, or up button on the front panel of the EV3 Intelligent Brick.

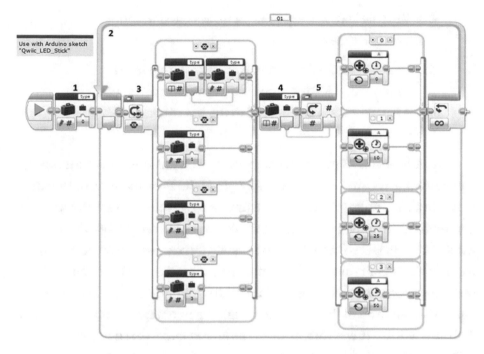

Figure 6-8. *EV3 program for selecting among three different analog outputs*

Steps in this program include

1. Variable Block: Declares a variable called type.

2. Loop Block: Sets up an infinite repetition of monitoring for a selection of one of the buttons on the EV3 Intelligent Brick front panel.

3. Switch—Brick Buttons Block: Assigns values to the variable type based on a button being pressed. If no button is pressed, then type is assigned a zero value. Pressing the left, right, or top button assigns a value of 1, 2, or 3, respectively, to type.

4. Variable Block: Reads the value assigned to the
    variable type.

5. Switch—Numeric: Assigns a power setting to an
    Unregulated Motor block connected to port A. Port
    A in this case is connected to the Breadboard
    Connector.

Running this EV3 program will produce the pulse-width modulation
waveforms of Figure 6-7 on the AN IN pin of the Breadboard Connector.
However, a DC voltage is required from these waveforms that the Arduino
can read on an analog input pin. This conversion from pulse-width
modulation to DC voltage is accomplished by passing the pulse-width
modulation signal through a low-pass filter based on an RC circuit. The
resulting DC voltage, connected to pin A0 on the Arduino, is shown in
Figure 6-9 for each of the three modulation percentages of Figure 6-7. The
Arduino will use these voltage levels as an indication to select among three
LED patterns to display, the subject of the following section.

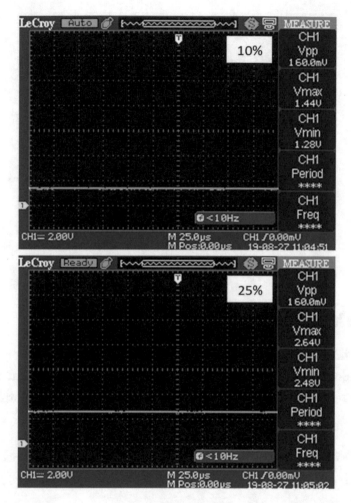

Figure 6-9. *The low-pass filter converts the pulse-width modulation input of Figure 6-7 to DC voltages shown here in these oscilloscope traces*

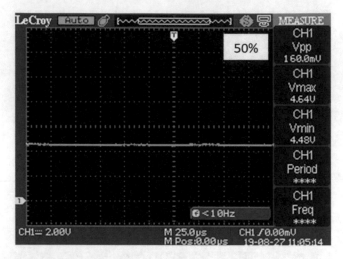

Figure 6-9. *(continued)*

Arduino Sketch

The function of the Arduino sketch, given in Listing 6-1, is to monitor for an analog voltage level input on pin A0. Depending on the measured voltage level, the Arduino will run one of the three possible algorithms for lighting the display on the Qwiic LED Stick.

Listing 6-1. The Arduino sketch for using the Qwiic LED Stick should be run at the same time as the EV3 program "LED_selector".

```
/*----------------------------------------------------
   LEGO LED Array
   Takes input from the front panel of the EV3 Intelligent Brick
   buttons to select LED patterns.
   LED patterns are displayed on a Qwiic LED Stick (sparkfun.com).
   Three patterns are programmed:
       Binary Counter at pressing EV3 left button.
       Walking Rainbow at pressing EV3 right button.
       Cycle Rainbow at pressing EV3 up button.
```

Communication from EV3 Intelligent Brick to Arduino is by analog voltages.

Wire connections:
    Qwiic red wire to Arduino 3.3 V
    Qwiic black wire to Arduino GND
    Qwiic blue wire to Arduino SDL
    Qwiic yellow wire to Arduino SCL
    EV3 breakout board VBUS to Arduino Vin
    EV3 breakout board Ain to RC circuit
    EV3 breakout board GRND (next to Ain) to Arduino GND
    EV3 breakout board SCL, SDA, VBUS, GRND (next to VBUS) to resistor circuit
    EV3 cable between Breadboard Connector and Port A on EV3 Intelligent Brick

Run program on EV3 Intelligent Brick called "LED_selector".

Qwiic LED Stick libraries and scripts copied from SparkFun link.
*/

```
#include <Wire.h>  //Call library for I2C communication between
Arduino and Qwiic LED stick
#include "Qwiic_LED_Stick.h" //Call library for Qwiic LED stick

LED LEDStick; //Create an object of the LED class

int input;  //Declare variable to test for input level

void setup() {
  Wire.begin();
  Serial.begin(9600);  //Start serial communication, used for
  diagnostic purposes.

  LEDStick.begin(); //Start up communication with the LED Stick

}
```

```
void loop() {

 LEDStick.LEDOff(); //Turn off all LEDs
 input = analogRead(A0); //Read voltage level coming from EV3
 Intelligent Brick

// Tests are run for three cases of voltage input, each in a
while loop.

 while( (input > 175) && (input < 275) ) {
     for (int i = 0; i < 1024; i++) {
       if ( (input > 275)  || (input < 175) )
       break;
       binaryLEDDisplay(i, 10);
     input = analogRead(A0);
     Serial.println(input); // Show input level on serial
                          monitor.
     delay(1000);
 }
 }
 while( (input > 400) && (input < 600) )  {
  if ( (input > 600) || (input < 400) )
  break;
  WalkingRainbow(20, 10, 50);
   input = analogRead(A0);
   Serial.println(input); // Show input level on serial monitor.

 }

 while(input > 600)  {
  if (input < 600)
  break;
  CycleRainbow(10);
```

```
  input = analogRead(AO);
  Serial.println(input); // Show input level on serial monitor.

 }
}

//------------------------------------------------------
//Functions follow for each of the three LED display
algorithms.

//Walks a rainbow of length rainbowLength across LED strip of
length LED Length with a delay of delayTime
//LEDLength<=rainbowLength<=255)
void WalkingRainbow(byte rainbowLength, byte LEDLength, int
delayTime) {
  //Create three LEDs the same length as the LEDStick to store
  color values
  byte redArray[LEDLength];
  byte greenArray[LEDLength];
  byte blueArray[LEDLength];
  //This will repeat rainbowLength times, generating 3 arrays
  (r,g,b) of length LEDLength
  //This is like creating rainbowLength different rainbow
  arrays where the positions
  //of each color have changed by 1
  for (byte j = 0; j < rainbowLength; j++) {
    //This will repeat LEDLength times, generating 3 colors
    (r,g,b) per pixel
    //This creates the array that is sent to the LED Stick
    for (byte i = 0 ; i < LEDLength ; i++) {
      //there are n colors generated for the rainbow
      //the rainbow starts at the location where i and j are
      equal: n=1
```

```
//the +1 accounts for the LEDs starting their index at 0
//the value of n determines which color is generated at
each pixel
int n = i + 1 - j;
//this will loop n so that n is always between 1 and
rainbowLength
if (n <= 0) {
  n = n + rainbowLength;
}
//the nth color is between red and yellow
if (n <= floor(rainbowLength / 6)) {
  redArray[i] = 255;
  greenArray[i] = floor(6 * 255 / (float) rainbowLength * n);
  blueArray[i] = 0;
}
//the nth color is between yellow and green
else if (n <= floor(rainbowLength / 3)) {
  redArray[i] = floor(510 - 6 * 255 / (float)
  rainbowLength * n);
  greenArray[i] = 255;
  blueArray[i] = 0;
}
//the nth color is between green and cyan
else if (n <= floor(rainbowLength / 2)) {
  redArray[i] = 0;
  greenArray[i] = 255;
  blueArray[i] = floor( 6 * 255 / (float) rainbowLength *
  n - 510);
}
//the nth color is between cyan and blue
```

```
    else if ( n <= floor(2 * rainbowLength / 3)) {
      redArray[i] = 0;
      greenArray[i] = floor(1020 - 6 * 255 / (float)
      rainbowLength * n);
      blueArray[i] = 255;
    }
    //the nth color is between blue and magenta
    else if (n <= floor(5 * rainbowLength / 6)) {
      redArray[i] = floor(6 * 255 / (float) rainbowLength *
      n - 1020);
      greenArray[i] = 0;
      blueArray[i] = 255;
    }
    //the nth color is between magenta and red
    else {
      redArray[i] = 255;
      greenArray[i] = 0;
      blueArray[i] = floor(1530 - (6 * 255 / (float)
      rainbowLength * n));;
    }
  }
  //sets all LEDs to the color values according to the arrays
  //the first LED corresponds to the first entries in the arrays
  LEDStick.setLEDColor(redArray, greenArray, blueArray,
  LEDLength);
  delay(delayTime);
  }
}
```

```
//Display binary on LEDS (LSB==LED10) of length LEDLength
void binaryLEDDisplay(int count, byte LEDLength) {
  //This for loop will repeat for each pixel of the LED Stick
  for (byte i = 0; i < LEDLength; i++) {
    //Below we use bit operators, which operate on the binary
    //representation of numbers. For ithBit, we use the
    //bitshift operator. count >> i takes the binary
    //representation of count and shifts it to the right i times.
    //For example,  if count was 10, 0b1010, and i was 2, we get
    //0b10. if i was 3, we get 0b1. This aligns the ith bit of
    //count to the 0th bit of ithBit byte ithBit = count >> i;
    //Here we use the bitwise and. This returns a 1 only in the
    //places where both operands have a 1. For example,
    //0b1011 & 0b1010 == 0b1010. Here we use 0b1 as an operand,
    //which means our output will be whatever the 0th bit of
    //ithBit is byte ithBitTrue = ithBit & 0b1; Here we write
    //to a single LED. We write only the color red, but you can
    //write to any combination of colors. We write to the (10-i)th
    //LED so that the last LED of your strip maps to bit 0 and
    //is the least significant bit, or the one's place. The value
    //for the color will be 255*ithBitTrue. Since ithBitTrue
    //can only be 1 or 0, we only send color values of either
    //255 or zero. This means that the (10-i)th LED will be red
    //if the ith bit of the count is 1, and will be off otherwise
    LEDStick.setLEDColor(10 - i, 255 * ithBitTrue, 0, 0);
  }
}

//Cycle through the rainbow with all LEDs the same color
void CycleRainbow(int delayTime) {
```

```
//will repeat for each color from red to yellow
for (byte g = 0; g < 255; g++) {
  //Set all LEDs to max red with green increasing each
  repetition
  LEDStick.setLEDColor(255, g, 0);
  delay(delayTime);
}

//will repeat for each color from yellow to green
for (byte r = 255; r > 0; r--) {
  //Set all LEDs to max green with red decreasing each
  repetition
  LEDStick.setLEDColor(r, 255, 0);
  delay(delayTime);

}

//will repeat for each color from green to cyan
for (byte b = 0; b < 255; b++) {
  //Set all LEDs to max green with blue increasing each
  repetition
  LEDStick.setLEDColor(0, 255, b);
  delay(delayTime);
}

//will repeat for each color from cyan to blue
for (byte g = 255; g > 0; g--) {
  //Set all LEDs to max blue with green decreasing each
  repetition
  LEDStick.setLEDColor(0, g, 255);
  delay(delayTime);
}
```

```
//will repeat for each color from blue to magenta
for (byte r = 0; r < 255; r++) {
  //Set all LEDs to max blue with red increasing each
  repetition
  LEDStick.setLEDColor(r, 0, 255);
  delay(delayTime);

}

//will repeat for each color from magenta to red

for (byte b = 255; b > 0; b--) {
  //Set all LEDs to max red with blue decreasing each
  repetition
  LEDStick.setLEDColor(255, 0, b);
  delay(delayTime);

}

}
```

Results

The brightness of the Qwiic LED Stick is impressive—it's sure to attract attention to displays. Videos of the three modes programmed in the preceding Arduino sketch can be seen at www.hightechlego.com. The brightness of the LEDs can be dialed down, if desired, by using lower values on the red/green/blue assignment. Full brightness values of 255 are used in the preceding sketch, which can be lowered.

Summary

In this chapter, a technique was developed to create an analog voltage output from the EV3 Intelligent Brick. The EV3 Intelligent Brick does not have a direct analog output, but instead has a pulse-width modulation output that can be converted to a DC level by a low-pass filter. An Arduino sketch was implemented to read the DC analog voltage signal to use as an indicator to execute various actions. These various actions were shown in an example application of selecting among three different LED patterns to play on a linear array of red/green/blue programmable LEDs. In the next chapter, a different technique will be developed for passing data between the EV3 Intelligent Brick and the Arduino.

CHAPTER 7

I2C Communication with the EV3 Intelligent Brick

The previous two chapters used an inter-integrated circuit (I2C) interface for a sensor to communicate with the Arduino. The Arduino sketches associated with these projects had the I2C setup built in by using Arduino sketches from sensor developers, so the user doesn't really get into details on the I2C operation. But I2C can also be used to communicate between the Arduino and the EV3 Intelligent Brick, passing bytes of data back and forth between the two devices. This chapter explores how to implement this I2C connection, based on a programming block built by Dexter Industries.

The EV3 I2C Block

Dexter Industries built an EV3 programming block that can read and write data over an I2C interface, available at `https://github.com/DexterInd/` `EV3_Dexter_Industries_Sensors` with a file called "Dexter.ev3b". This file then gets imported into the MINDSTORMS EV3 programming environment as per the directions of Chapter 2. Several new programming blocks appear, corresponding to the aftermarket MINDSTORMS-compatible sensors made by Dexter Industries. One of these new blocks allows for I2C communication, as pictured in Figure 7-1.

© Grady Koch 2020

G. Koch, *The LEGO Arduino Cookbook*, https://doi.org/10.1007/978-1-4842-6303-7_7

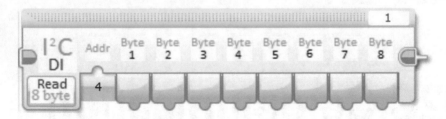

Figure 7-1. *The I2C block allows for passing 8 bytes of data*

The projects in this book use the option for either reading or writing 8 bytes of data, selected in the pull-down menu setting with the "Read 8 byte" option shown in Figure 7-1. The port over which data will be connected is in the upper-right corner, as it is for all the other EV3 sensor blocks, with the example of Figure 7-1 set for port 1. Another setting is the device address, labeled "Addr" in the programming block and set to 4 in Figure 7-1, which must match the address used in the Arduino sketch used at the same time—examples of Arduino address setting will be shown in the following chapters. Eight data ports, labeled "Byte 1" to "Byte 8," provide access for using data read into the EV3 Intelligent Brick. The interpretation of these bytes is described in the following section.

Bits and Bytes

Data passed over I2C is in the form of a number represented by one byte. A byte, in this design, is comprised of 8 bits, with a bit being a binary digit representing either a 0 or a 1. Of these 8 bits, 7 bits indicate a number value to transfer, and 1 bit indicates if the number is positive or negative. So an example 7-bit number field could be 1101011. The I2C programming block of Figure 7-1 translates each 7-bit byte into a decimal number equivalent, with each bit representing if a power of 2 is involved as per the example of Table 7-1 that finds the decimal equivalent of the byte example 1101011.

Table 7-1. *The I2C programming block of Figure 7-1 converts a byte to a decimal equivalent by adding up powers of 2*

Bit Number	Value (If Bit Is 1)	Exponent Equivalent for the Example Byte of 1101011
0 (rightmost bit)	1	1
1	2	2
2	4	0
3	8	8
4	16	0
5	32	32
6 (leftmost bit)	64	64

The decimal equivalent is found by adding up all the exponent equivalents, the third column in Table 7-1. So for the example byte of 1101011, the decimal equivalent is 64+32+0+8+0+2+1=107.

The I2C programming block of Figure 7-1 does the byte-to-decimal conversion automatically, so there is no need for the user to get involved in the calculation. However, the use of 7-bit fields has a consequence in writing software programs, in that using this 7-bit field means that only a number up to 1+2+4+8+16+32+64=127 can be represented. There's no way, using this one field, to represent a number greater than 127. Actually, there's an 8th bit involved that the sign of the number representation can be made of a number of –127 to 127 when writing from the Arduino.

If a number outside the range of –127 to 127 is involved, then extra manipulation will be required in the software program, perhaps involving more than one byte. Similarly, if a more precise number is needed, with numbers after a decimal point, then creativity is needed in representing numbers. These special cases will be seen in the projects of the following chapters.

Wiring Connections

Data transfer is made over I2C over a wiring connection of the Breadboard Connector described in Chapter 1, pictured in Figure 1-7. There are two sets of wiring connections to make. One set of connections, diagrammed in Figure 7-2, is by an EV3 cable between the EV3 Intelligent Brick and the Breadboard Connector. The second set of connections, diagrammed in Figure 7-3, involves four jumper wires from the Breadboard Connector to the Arduino.

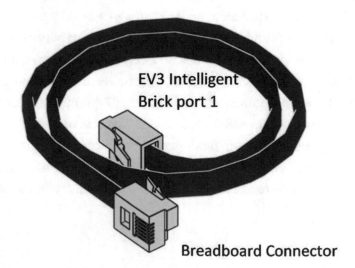

Figure 7-2. *A Connector Cable links the EV3 Intelligent Brick to the Breadboard Connector*

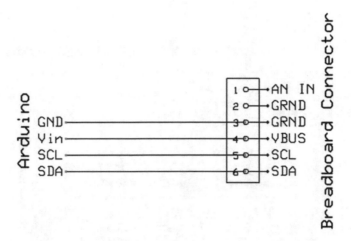

Figure 7-3. *Connection of the Arduino to I2C involves four jumper wires*

Reading Bytes into the EV3 Intelligent Brick

A utility of I2C used in several projects in the following chapters is to pass data from the Arduino to the EV3 Intelligent Brick. The Dexter Industries I2C block can be used to accomplish this as per the EV3 program code in the following section. To demonstrate data transfer, an Arduino sketch is also given in a following section. Numeric data assigned in the Arduino sketch is passed to the EV3 Intelligent Brick for display on its front panel.

EV3 Code for Reading

The EV3 program for reading data into the EV3 Intelligent Brick is shown in Figure 7-4. To keep the figure small enough to fit onto the page, only 2 bytes of data are being displayed from the I2C block—the remaining 6 bytes could be read and manipulated in a similar way as the first 2. Steps in the program include

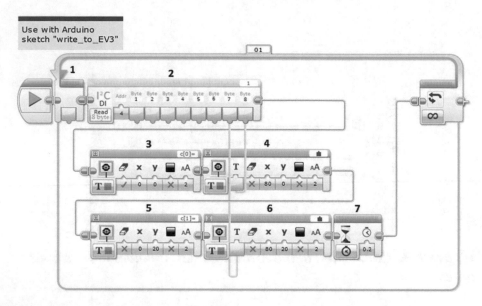

Figure 7-4. *EV3 code for reading over I2C is based on the Dexter Industries I2C programming block*

1. Loop Block: Sets up an infinite repetition of reading and displaying data.

2. I2C Block: Reads 8 bytes of data over address 4. Only byte numbers 7 and 8 are being read and displayed in this example. The byte order is reversed from what is being sent by the Arduino, with the first byte sent by the Arduino loaded into byte number 8 of the I2C block.

3. Display Block: Prints a label of "c[0]" on the front panel to indicate the value being displayed in block 4.

4. Display Block: Prints the value transferred over I2C as byte 8. This value is loaded into the c array as the first value, c[0].

5. Display Block: Prints a label of "c[1]" on the front
    panel to indicate the value being displayed in block 4.

6. Display Block: Prints the value transferred over I2C
    as byte 8. This value is loaded into the c array as the
    second value, c[1].

7. Wait Block: Pauses the program to avoid an overflow
    of data being read into the EV3 Intelligent Brick.

Arduino Sketch for Writing

The Arduino sketch, given in Listing 7-1, sends an array of 8 bytes over
I2C to the EV3 Intelligent Brick. The bytes sent are values assigned in the
sketch, which in later projects will be variables associated with data, such
as parameters measured by a sensor.

Listing 7-1. The Arduino sketch for writing from the Arduino to
the EV3 Intelligent Brick should be run at the same time as the EV3
program "EV3_read"

```
/*-----------------------------------------------------
Reading Bytes into the EV3 Intelligent Brick

This sketch passes an array of data from the Arduino to the
EV3 Intelligent Brick.  The array is called c[], with 8 values
assigned in the script below.

Connections:
EV3 Breadboard VBUS to Arduino VIN
EV3 Breadboard GRND (next to VBUS) to Arduino GND
EV3 Breadboard SCL to Arduino SCL
EV3 Breadboard SDA to Arduino SDA
```

EV3 cable between breadboard connector and Port 1 of EV3 Intelligent Brick

Use with EV3 program "EV3_read"

Arduino to EV3 connection modified from Dexter Industries post www.dexterindustries.com/howto/connecting-ev3-arduino

```
-----------------------------------------------------*/

#include <Wire.h>  //Call library for I2C communications

#define SLAVE_ADDRESS 0x04  //I2C address for communicating
with EV3 Intelligent
//Brick.  Same address should be in EV3 program

byte c[]={10,11,12,13,14,15,16,17}; //Declare array that will
be sent to EV3
//Intelligent Brick.

void setup()
{
  Serial.begin(9600);  //Start serial communications.  Serial
  monitor must match this baud rate.
  Wire.begin(SLAVE_ADDRESS); //Start I2C link
  Serial.println("Writing values to the EV3 Intelligent Brick . . .");

}

void loop()
{

  Wire.onRequest(sendData); //Send data to EV3
  delay(100);
}
```

```
//Function for sending data.
void sendData()
{
  Wire.write(c,8); //c is the array of 8 bytes length
}
```

Writing Bytes from the EV3 Intelligent Brick

The previous sections described moving data from the Arduino into the
EV3 Intelligent Brick, but data can also go the other way to write data from
the EV3 Intelligent Brick. The software programs for writing from the EV3
are similar to reading into the EV3, as can be seen in the following section.
The same EV3 programming block is used for writing as for reading; the
difference is in a menu selection in the programming block.

EV3 Code for Writing

The EV3 program for writing data over I2C is shown in Figure 7-5, using the
Dexter Industries I2C block. In this example, the 8 bytes have been loaded
with values ranging from 1 to 8. When writing from the EV3 Intelligent
Brick, only positive values are allowed, so the possible range of numbers is
0 to 127. These values could, of course, instead be sensor data from various
MINDSTORMS sensors. Steps in this EV3 code include

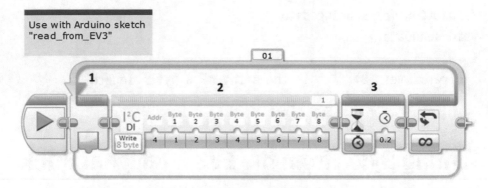

Figure 7-5. *EV3 code for writing data from the EV3 Intelligent Brick over I2C uses the Dexter Industries programming block*

1. Loop Block: Sets up an infinite repetition of writing data.

2. I2C Block: Writes 8 bytes of data over address 4.

3. Wait Block: Pauses action by 0.2 seconds to avoid an overflow of data being sent to the Arduino.

Arduino Sketch for Reading

The Arduino sketch, shown in Listing 7-2, for reading in data from the EV3 has an array of 8 bytes loaded with numerical values. Each byte can be a number from 0 to 127. Dummy values are loaded into the EV3 program for this example program. But these values can represent sensor data to pass to the Arduino, as will be seen in Chapter 11.

Listing 7-2. The Arduino sketch for reading from the EV3 Intelligent Brick to the Arduino should be run at the same time as the EV3 program "EV3_write"

```
/*----------------------------------------------------
Writing Bytes from the EV3 Intelligent Brick

This sketch passes an array of data from the EV3 Intelligent
Brick to the Arduino.  The array is called d[], with 8 values
assigned in the script below.  The values are displayed on the
serial monitor.

Connections:
EV3 Breadboard VBUS to Arduino VIN
EV3 Breadboard GRND (next to VBUS) to Arduino GND
EV3 Breadboard SCL to Arduino SCL
EV3 Breadboard SDA to Arduino SDA
EV3 cable between breadboard connector and Port 1 of EV3
Intelligent Brick

Use with EV3 program "EV3_write"

Arduino to EV3 connection modified from Dexter Industries post
www.dexterindustries.com/howto/connecting-ev3-arduino

----------------------------------------------------*/

#include <Wire.h>  //Call library for I2C communications

#define SLAVE_ADDRESS 0x04  //I2C address for communicating
with EV3 Intelligent
//Brick.  Same address should be in EV3 program
```

```
void setup()
{
    Serial.begin(9600); //Start serial communications.
    Serial monitor must match this baud rate.
    Wire.begin(SLAVE_ADDRESS);  //Start I2C link
    Wire.onReceive(receiveData); //Read data from EV3
    Serial.println("Ready!");
}
int val,flag=0,index=0;
byte d[]={10,11,12,13,14,15,16,17};  //dCeclare array to be
                                        sent to the Arduino

int i; //declare loop increment

void loop()
{
 Serial.println(d[0]);  //Send values to serial monitor.
 Serial.println(d[1]);
 Serial.println(d[2]);
 Serial.println(d[3]);
 Serial.println(d[4]);
 Serial.println(d[5]);
 Serial.println(d[6]);
 Serial.println(d[7]);
 delay(500);
}

//Function for reading data.
void receiveData(int byteCount)
{
    i=0;
    while(Wire.available()>0)
        {
```

```
    val=Wire.read();
    d[i]=val;
    i = i + 1;
    flag=1;

  }

}
```

I2C Conflicts

While the I2C interface can allow for multiple sensors to be connected to an Arduino, problems arise when using I2C for both Arduino-to-sensor and Arduino-to-EV3 communications. Conflicts occur in the I2C signals if this dual-use communication is tried. So, in all the projects of this book, I2C is only used for Arduino-to-sensor or Arduino-to-EV3. In the case of using Arduino-to-EV3 I2C communications, a different interface is used for Arduino-to-sensor, such as PWM or SPI.

Summary

An I2C interface can pass numerical data between the Arduino and the EV3 Intelligent Brick, facilitated by an I2C programming block built by Dexter Industries. The data is structured to pass 8 bytes of data at one time, with each byte representing an integer number of absolute value up to 127. When reading into the EV3 Intelligent Brick, a positive or negative number can be represented for a range of –127 to +127. But when writing from the EV3 Intelligent Brick, only positive numbers can be represented from 0 to 127. The EV3 code and sketches developed in this chapter will be used in the following chapters, passing sensor data between the Arduino and the EV3 Intelligent Brick.

CHAPTER 8

The LEGO Lidar— PWM Sensor with EV3 I2C Interface

A lidar is a device for measuring distance using a pulsed laser. The name is an acronym for "light detection and ranging." An optical receiver in the lidar looks for the laser pulse reflected from objects in the laser beam. By relating the time delay between the transmission and reception of the pulse to the speed of light, distance can be measured. The laser light from lidars is typically infrared and so is not visible to the human eye. Lidars for distance measurement have been around for a while, but until recently have been either too expensive or too limited in capability to be of much interest. However, a breakthrough device came out that measures to a useful distance (40 m) at a reasonable cost (US\$130), called the LIDAR-Lite v3 made by Garmin and available at `www.sparkfun.com`, `www.robotshop.com`, and `www.amazon.com`. The LIDAR-Lite v3 is pictured in Figure 8-1. In this chapter, a design will be presented for mounting the lidar, scanning it with a LEGO motor, and controlling it with the EV3 Intelligent Brick. Two versions of the control code are presented: one for 10-m distance capability at 1-cm resolution and another for 40-m distance capability at 4-cm resolution. Several applications for the LEGO Lidar will be shown for scanning for intruders, measuring the dimensions of trees, and monitoring roadway traffic.

© Grady Koch 2020
G. Koch, *The LEGO Arduino Cookbook*, https://doi.org/10.1007/978-1-4842-6303-7_8

Figure 8-1. *The LIDAR-Lite v3 has two optical ports: one for transmitting the laser pulse and one for receiving reflections*

Mounting the Lidar

As shown in Figure 8-2, a 1 x 6 Technic Brick with Holes can be glued onto the base of the LIDAR-Lite v3 for mounting purposes. Cyanoacrylate glue, such as Krazy Glue, Gorilla Glue, or Super Glue, works well for this attachment. Then the lidar can be attached to an EV3 Large Motor by Technic Pins, which allows the lidar beam to be scanned in angle. The complete LEGO Lidar setup is shown in Figure 8-3.

Figure 8-2. *A Technic brick glued onto the base of the LIDAR-Lite v3 gives a means for attachment to LEGO*

Figure 8-3. *The complete LEGO Lidar includes a motorized control for scanning the lidar beam*

Accommodation of the motor mount for the LIDAR-Lite v3 is given in the following building steps. This motor mount can then be attached to the LEGO Arduino Workstation, as can be seen in Figure 8-3.

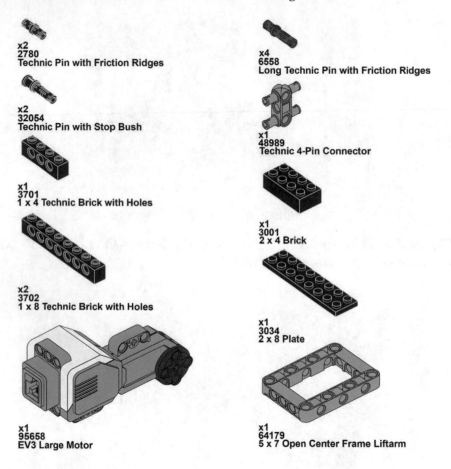

x2
2780
Technic Pin with Friction Ridges

x2
32054
Technic Pin with Stop Bush

x1
3701
1 x 4 Technic Brick with Holes

x2
3702
1 x 8 Technic Brick with Holes

x1
95658
EV3 Large Motor

x4
6558
Long Technic Pin with Friction Ridges

x1
48989
Technic 4-Pin Connector

x1
3001
2 x 4 Brick

x1
3034
2 x 8 Plate

x1
64179
5 x 7 Open Center Frame Liftarm

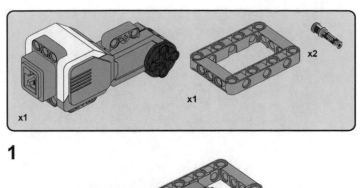

1

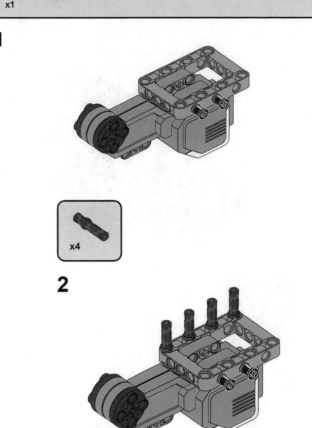

2

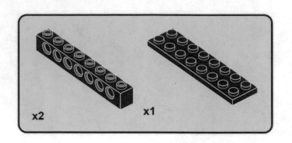

3

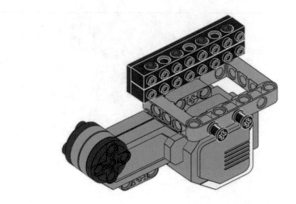

4

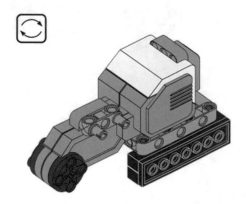

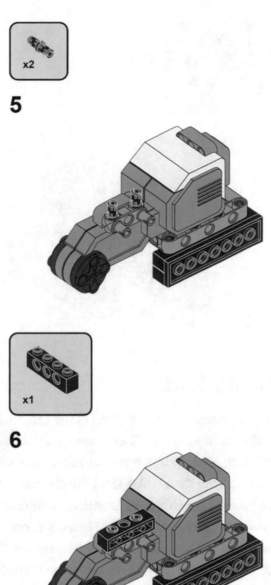

5

6

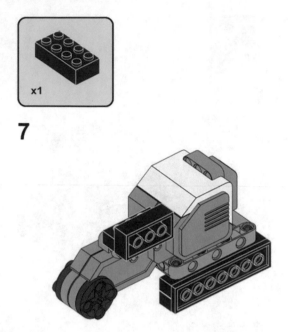

7

Wiring Connections

Four sets of wiring connections are needed: (1) the LIDAR-Lite v3 to Arduino, (2) Arduino to Breadboard Connector, (3) Breadboard Connector to EV3 Intelligent Brick, and (4) EV3 Intelligent Brick to EV3 Large Motor. Electronic connection from the LIDAR-Lite v3 to the Arduino is by a cable supplied with the lidar. This cable is of six wires in colors of red, orange, yellow, green, blue, and black. As shown in Figure 8-4, only the red, black, and yellow wires will be used in the design of this chapter that makes use of the pulse-width modulation (PWM) output of the LIDAR-Lite v3. The PWM connection requires a resistor of 1-kΩ, which can be inserted into the breadboard of the LEGO Arduino Workstation as diagrammed in the schematic of Figure 8-4.

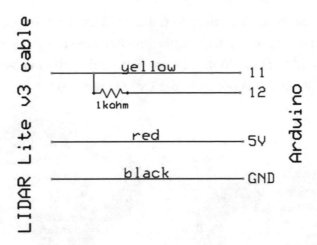

Figure 8-4. *Connection between the LIDAR-Lite v3 and Arduino involves three wires of the lidar's cable*

The second set of wire connections links the Arduino to the EV3 Intelligent Brick via the Breadboard Connector Adapter for I2C communications. These connections are diagrammed in Figure 8-5. This connection will pass measurements of distance to the EV3 Intelligent Brick.

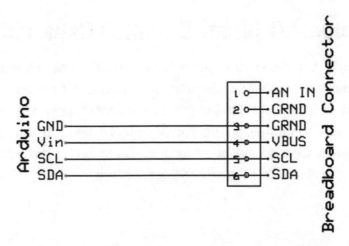

Figure 8-5. *Communication between the Arduino and the EV3 Intelligent Brick is by I2C*

115

The third and fourth connections are by EV3 Connector Cables, as diagrammed in Figure 8-6. One cable goes between the EV3 Intelligent Brick port 4 and the Breadboard Connector. And another cable connects the EV3 Intelligent Brick port A to the EV3 Large Motor.

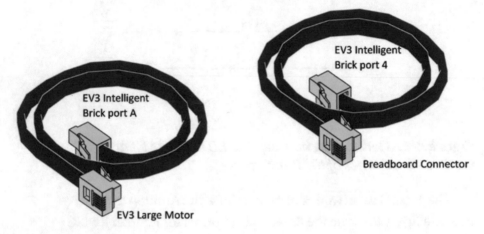

Figure 8-6. *A Connector Cable links the EV3 Intelligent Brick to the Breadboard Connector*

EV3 Code: 10-Meter Distance Capability

The EV3 program, shown in Figure 8-7, uses an I2C block to bring in distance measurements from the lidar. As explained in Chapter 7, this block reads in 8 bytes at a time, with each 8-bit byte representing a number from 0 to 127 in centimeters. The sum of these 8 bytes is the total distance in centimeters, so they must be added together in the EV3 program. Programming blocks serve the following functions:

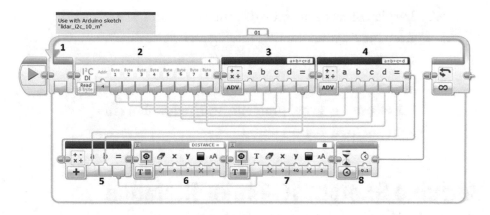

Figure 8-7. *EV3 program for reading measurements from the Arduino*

1. Loop Block: Sets up an infinite loop to measure and report distance measurements from the lidar.

2. I2C Block: Reads 8 bytes of data sent by the Arduino. The Arduino is connected via a Breadboard Connector to port 4 of the EV3 Intelligent Brick. The Addr setting is at 4 to match the address set in the Arduino code that runs the same time as this EV3 program.

3. Math Block: Adds together the values of bytes 1 through 4 read from the I2C block.

4. Math Block: Adds together the values of bytes 5 through 8 read from the I2C block.

5. Math Block: Adds together the results of blocks 3 and 4.

6. Display Block: Prints a label on the EV3 Intelligent Brick's display to serve as a reminder of what is being measured.

117

7. Display Block: Prints the distance measurements from the lidar on the EV3 Intelligent Brick's display in units of centimeters.

8. Wait Block: Delays the measurement repetition by 0.1 seconds to avoid problems with overpolling the Arduino for a measurement.

Arduino Sketch: 10-Meter Distance Capability

The sketch to run on the Arduino, shown in Listing 8-1, reads the pulse-width modulation output from the LIDAR-Lite v3, in which the length of the pulse is proportional to distance. I2C communication is set up between the Arduino, described in detail in Chapter 7, to pass measurement results upon request from the EV3 Intelligent Brick. If the Arduino is connected to a desktop computer, the lidar measurement results can also be seen in the Arduino IDE Serial Monitor.

Listing 8-1. The Arduino sketch for measuring up to 10-m distance with the LIDAR-Lite v3 should be run at the same time as the EV3 program "lidar_10_m"

```
/*-----------------------------------------------------
  LEGO Lidar
  Takes measurements from Garmin Lidar-Lite V3 and tranfers
  data to EV3 Intelligent Brick.
  Measurements are valid to 10-m of distance with 1-cm resolution.
  Lidar-Lite V3 mode of operation is with pulse width modulation.
  Communication between EV3 Intelligent Brick and Arduino is
  by I2C.
```

Connections:

LIDAR-Lite 5 Vdc (red) to Arduino 5v

LIDAR-Lite Ground (black) to Arduino GND

LIDAR-Lite Mode control (yellow) to Arduino digital input (pin 11)

LIDAR-Lite Mode control (yellow) to 1 kOhm resistor lead 1

1 kOhm resistor lead 2 to Arduino digital output (pin 12)

EV3 Breadboard Connector VBUS to Arduino Vin

EV3 Breadboard Connector GRND (next to VBUS) to Arduino GND

EV3 Breadboard Connector SCL to Arduino SCL

EV3 Breadboard Connector SDA to Arduino SDA

EV3 cable between Breadboard Connector and Port 4 of EV3 Intelligent Brick

Run program on EV3 Intelligent Brick called "lidar_10_m".

See the Operation Manual for wiring diagrams and more information:
http://static.garmin.com/pumac/LIDAR_Lite_v3_Operation_Manual_and_Technical_Specifications.pdf

Arduino to EV3 connection modified from Dexter Industries post
www.dexterindustries.com/howto/connecting-ev3-arduino
--*/
#include <Wire.h> //Call Library for I2C communications.

#define SLAVE_ADDRESS 0x04 //I2C address for communicating with EV3 Intelligent Brick. Same address should be in EV3 program.

unsigned long pulseWidth; //Declare variable of pulse width measured from lidar.
unsigned long distance; //Declare variable of distance, related to pulse width.

```
byte c[]={10,11,12,13,14,15,16,17};   //Declaring array that
                                         will be sent to EV3
                                         Intelligent Brick.  Loaded
                                         with dummy values that can
                                         help de-bugging.

void setup()
{
  Serial.begin(9600); //Start serial communications.  Serial
  monitor must match this baud rate.

  pinMode(12, OUTPUT); //Set pin 12 as trigger pin.
  digitalWrite(12, LOW); //Set trigger LOW for continuous read.

  pinMode(11, INPUT); //Set pin 11 as monitor pin.

  Wire.begin(SLAVE_ADDRESS);

}

void loop()
{
  pulseWidth = pulseIn(11, HIGH); //Count how long the pulse is
                                    high in microseconds.
  distance = pulseWidth / 10; //10usec = 1 cm of distance.

  if (distance <= 127) { //Test for range of values. Repeated
                          in if statements below.
    c[0] = 0;
    c[1] = 0;
    c[2] = 0;
    c[3] = 0;
    c[4] = 0;
    c[5] = 0;
```

```
  c[6] = 0;
  c[7] = distance;
}

if (distance > 127 && distance <= 254) {
  c[0] = 0;
  c[1] = 0;
  c[2] = 0;
  c[3] = 0;
  c[4] = 0;
  c[5] = 0;
  c[6] = distance - 127;
  c[7] = 127;
}

  if (distance > 254 && distance <= 381) {
  c[0] = 0;
  c[1] = 0;
  c[2] = 0;
  c[3] = 0;
  c[4] = 0;
  c[5] = distance - 254;
  c[6] = 127;
  c[7] = 127;
}

if (distance > 381 && distance <= 508) {
  c[0] = 0;
  c[1] = 0;
  c[2] = 0;
  c[3] = 0;
  c[4] = distance - 381;
```

```
    c[5] = 127;
    c[6] = 127;
    c[7] = 127;
  }

  if (distance > 508 && distance <= 635) {
    c[0] = 0;
    c[1] = 0;
    c[2] = 0;
    c[3] = distance - 508;
    c[4] = 127;
    c[5] = 127;
    c[6] = 127;
    c[7] = 127;
  }

  if (distance > 635 && distance <= 762) {
    c[0] = 0;
    c[1] = 0;
    c[2] = distance - 635;
    c[3] = 127;
    c[4] = 127;
    c[5] = 127;
    c[6] = 127;
    c[7] = 127;
  }

    if (distance > 762 && distance <= 889) {
    c[0] = 0;
    c[1] = distance - 762;
    c[2] = 127;
    c[3] = 127;
    c[4] = 127;
    c[5] = 127;
```

```
    c[6] = 127;
    c[7] = 127;
  }

    if (distance > 889 && distance <= 1016) {
    c[0] = distance - 889;
    c[1] = 127;
    c[2] = 127;
    c[3] = 127;
    c[4] = 127;
    c[5] = 127;
    c[6] = 127;
    c[7] = 127;
  }

    Serial.println(distance); //Print the distance to Arduino
                              serial monitor.
    Wire.onRequest(sendData); //Send data to EV3

}

//Function for sending data.
void sendData()
{
  Wire.write(c,8); //c is the array of 8 bytes length.
}
```

Software Modification for 40-Meter Distance Capability

The code in the previous section works with measurements up to a 10-meter distance with a maximum possible resolution of 1 cm. The working distance can be extended to the full capability of the lidar

(40 m) at the expense of resolution. The technique for doing so is
a simple approach of scaling the measurements from the lidar by a
factor of 4 so that the range of values can fit within the 8 bytes allowed
by the I2C programming block in the EV3. To remove the scaling, the
measurements transferred into the EV3 are multiplied by a factor of 4.
Figure 8-8 shows the EV3 program to work up to 40-m distance, with
the change highlighted from the 10-m program of Figure 8-7. The
difference in the programs is just a Math block to multiply by 4.

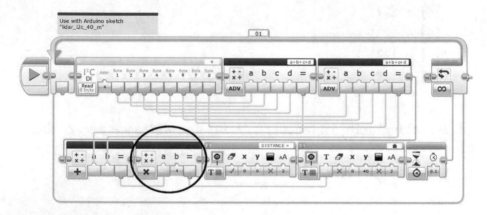

Figure 8-8. *A multiplication by 4 is needed to accommodate lidar
measurement beyond 10-m distance*

The Arduino script also needs a modification to work with distance
values to 40 meters, accomplished with a one-line change in code. This
change is

```
distance = pulseWidth / 10; //10usec = 1 cm of distance
```

to

```
distance = pulseWidth / 40; //10usec = 1 cm of distance, with
                                    scaling by 4.
```

This modified sketch should be saved as `lidar_i2c_40_m`.

Example Application: Scanning a Scene

The first step in working with the LEGO Lidar is to decide on the distance to which measurements will be made: less than 10 meters or more than 10 meters. Two versions of the EV3 program and Arduino sketches were developed earlier for these two options. In the applications described here, an assumption is made that the targets can be at a distance of no more than 40 meters. The Arduino sketch would then be loaded with lidar_ i2c_40_m. Various applications of the LEGO Lidar are then programmed with EV3 software. Programs are simplified by making a My Block of the blocks that read data from the Arduino and apply math functions to create a distance measurement. The programming blocks gathered into a My Block are illustrated in Figure 8-9—a parameter called "a" is output from this block of the lidar distance measurement.

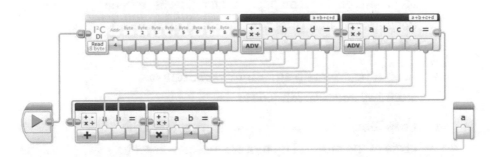

Figure 8-9. *A My Block can be created of the lidar measurement*

This My Block can then be used in a variety of programs, such as the one in Figure 8-10, to scan the lidar to view a sector of 120 degrees in azimuth. The motor is moved incrementally by 1 degree, taking a distance measurement at each increment. Scan angles and distances are recorded onto the EV3 Intelligent Brick for later download and analysis. Steps in this program include

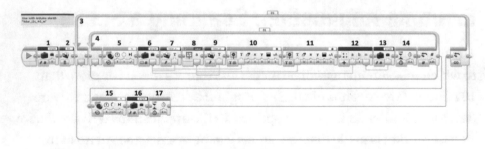

Figure 8-10. *EV3 code for scanning the lidar involves control of an EV3 Large Motor*

1. Variable Block: Declares a variable called `angle` to represent the angle at which the lidar is pointing.

2. File Access Block: Declares and deletes previous data of a file name called `lidar scan` to fill with angle and distance measurements. This file will be downloaded after program execution to view and plot data.

3. Loop Block: Sets up an infinite repetition of scanning and recording data.

4. Loop Block: Repeats 120 times to increment the angle of the motor. The motor angle gets reset to a starting point after the loop runs through to 120 iterations. The value of 120 could be changed if a different sector angle is desired.

5. Large Motor Block: Moves the motor by 1 degree. The power on the motor is kept low, at a value of 5, to avoid overshooting the small increase in angle.

6. Variable Block: Reads the current value of `angle`.

7. File Access Block: Records the `angle` value to the `lidar scan` file.

8. Lidar Block: Uses the My Block of Figure 8-9 to read a measurement from the LIDAR-Lite v3.

9. File Access Block: Records the distance measurement to the `lidar scan` file. Each new value recorded to the file is appended at the end of the file.

10. Display Block: Prints the current angle setting on the display of the EV3 Intelligent Brick.

11. Display Block: Prints the current distance measurement on the display of the EV3 Intelligent Brick. This distance value appears underneath the angle value on the display.

12. Math Block: Increments the value of the variable `angle` by 1 degree.

13. Variable Block: Stores the new value of the variable `angle`.

14. Wait Block: Pauses the program for 0.1 seconds.

15. Large Motor Block: Resets the motor position back to its start point after the scanning loop is complete. The angle entered should be the negative of the value used in block 4.

16. Variable Block: Resets the `angle` variable back to zero.

17. Wait Block: Pauses program operation for 0.1 seconds.

An example application of the program of Figure 8-10 is shown in Figure 8-11, where the lidar was used to scan a view of a residential yard. A photograph of this backyard area is shown in Figure 8-12. Two scans of the lidar are shown. One scan, drawn in green, is of normal features of the area including bushes, a swing set, play fort, tree, and a garden shed. The second scan, drawn in blue, indicates something unusual has entered the scene, showing that the lidar can be used as a security system for detecting intruders. A relatively long wide-angle scan was made in this example, but the scan time could be quickened by scanning just a few angles that could be a likely path for intrusion.

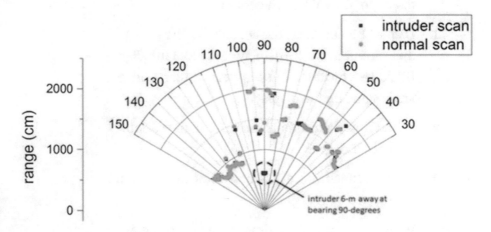

Figure 8-11. *The lidar can monitor for intrusion into an area, in this case the yard seen in the photograph in Figure 8-12*

Figure 8-12. *The bushes, swing set, play fort, trees, and a shed are picked up in the lidar scan of Figure 8-11*

Example Application: Measuring Trees

Whereas the LEGO Lidar was used to scan in azimuth in the previous section, it can also be turned on its side to scan in elevation, as shown in Figure 8-13. One use for the elevation-scanning lidar is to measure the dimensions of trees. Such measurements are important for studies in forestry and ecology, with the height of a tree and the dimensions of the leaf canopy giving insight on the health, age, and biomass content of a tree. To demonstrate this measurement, the tree pictured in Figure 8-14 was scanned in height. The program of Figure 8-10 was changed in setting for this experiment with the angular extent entered to 70 degrees in blocks 4 and 15. The starting angle of zero degrees was set to be horizontal.

Figure 8-13. *The LEGO Lidar can be set on its side to scan in elevation, with LEGO bricks added on the sides to give stability*

The result of the scan is shown in Figure 8-15 in a polar plot. With the lidar aimed by hand in azimuth to hit the horizontal center line of the tree, the vertical extent of the tree is clearly seen as a scan in elevation is executed. Several conclusions can be made from this data: (1) the height of the tree is 24.9m × sin (49°) = 18.8 meters, (2) the leafy canopy extends from a height of 3 meters to 18.8 meters, and (3) the diameter of the canopy at the widest point, called *crown spread*, is 15 meters. Scanning the tree multiple times allows for occasional lidar pulses to view through leaves and branches from minor variation of the scan angle and from wind stirring the leaves of the tree.

Figure 8-14. *This tree was scanned in height, with results shown in Figure 8-15*

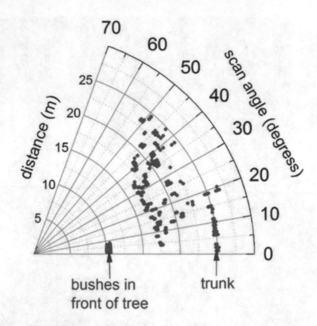

Figure 8-15. *The lidar scan of the tree shows the dimensions, including canopy structure*

Adding a Camera: The LEGO Traffic Monitor

An interesting additional capability can be added to the LEGO Lidar by aligning a camera to the lidar beam, as has been done in Figure 8-16. A photograph or video can be recorded at the same time a scene is being scanned. Or if the lidar detects the presence of something, the scene can be captured with images. For example, an intruder detected by the setup of an earlier section in this chapter could be recorded on video. As another example, the LEGO Lidar can monitor traffic passing on a roadway. A record can be made of the number of vehicles or pedestrians that use a road, in which direction they are traveling, and the speed of their motion.

Figure 8-16. *A camera and lidar can be coaligned to correlate distance measurements with imagery*

The camera used in this setup is a LEGO-compatible device made by Mindsensors.com called Vision Subsystem v5. This camera has a lens that can be removed and replaced with other lenses, if, as has been done here, a wider field of view is desired. Compatible lenses are in a mount called M12, such as those made by Arducam (`www.arducam.com`). A lens of 120-degree horizontal field of view is shown installed in Figure 8-16.

The Vision Subsystem v5 has an EV3 programming block associated with it, downloadable from `www.mindsensors.com`. This block has been put to use in the EV3 program shown in Figure 8-17. In this example program, the motor is not controlled to scan the lidar beam so no motor control blocks appear in the program. Steps in this program include

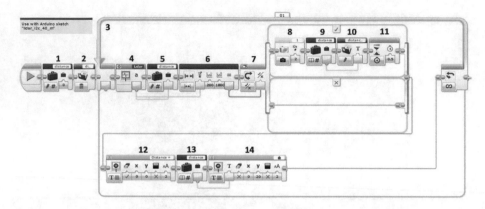

Figure 8-17. *EV3 code for the LEGO Traffic Monitor stores both images and distance measurements*

1. Variable Block: Declares a variable called `distance` to represent the distance measured by the lidar.

2. File Access Block: Declares and deletes a file name called `distance log` to fill with distance measurements. This file will be downloaded after program execution to view and plot data.

3. Loop Block: Sets up an infinite repetition of measuring distance to determine if a vehicle, pedestrian, or other object is in the lidar's beam.

4. Lidar Block: Uses the My Block of Figure 8-9 to read a measurement from the LIDAR-Lite v3.

5. Variable Block: Stores the lidar's distance measurement to the variable `distance`.

6. Range Block: Determines if the distance measured is between the value of 200 and 1800 centimeters.

7. Switch Block: Presents true and false paths based on the boolean outcome of the Range block. If a target is detected, then blocks 8 to 11 are executed. If no target is detected, then no action is taken as directed by the false path of the Switch.

8. Mindsensors NXTCam5 Block: Takes a picture with the Vision Subsystem v5 camera. The image file gets stored onto the SD card that is part of the Vision Subsystem v5—images are downloaded later. There is some delay involved between when the command is given and when the image is taken, found in testing to be 1 second.

9. Variable Block: Reads the distance variable.

10. File Access Block: Writes the distance measurement to the file distance log. Images can then be correlated with the distance measured by the lidar.

11. Wait Block: Delays action by ½ second to avoid repeating a photograph and distance measurement on the same target.

12. Display Block: Prints a label on the front panel of the EV3 Intelligent Brick as a reminder of the quantity being displayed in the next block.

13. Variable Block: Recalls the value of the distance variable.

14. Display Block: Prints the latest distance measurement on the front panel of the EV3 Intelligent Brick. This value gets updated when the next target is identified.

An example image of a car viewed with this traffic monitor is shown in Figure 8-18. The lidar is pointed to the center of the image, but since the car is in motion and the camera has a 1-second delay in taking a photograph, the car appears well off-center. This movement was the motivation for picking a wide field of view for the camera at 120 degrees. Otherwise, with a more standard field of view, the car would have been out of the frame of the image. The position of the car in the image indicates the vehicle's speed. Speed was calibrated in this setup by driving a car through the lidar beam at known speed of 25 mph. This speed was found to place the front bumper of the car at a particular place in the image, such as in the example of Figure 8-18. Cars appearing beyond this location in the field of view were then known to be exceeding the legal speed limit of 25 mph for this residential road. Statistics could be found for the number of cars exceeding speed limit—about 30% of drivers exceeded the speed limit by at least 3 mph.

Figure 8-18. *A car is photographed and measured for speed after triggering the LEGO Traffic Monitor*

Summary

A lidar allows precise measurements of distance that can be applied to determining dimensions of distant objects, detecting intruders, and triggering other devices. The LIDAR-Lite v3 provides distance measurement to targets up to about 40 meters. The interface of the LIDAR-Lite v3 can be made by the pulse-width modulation output of the lidar connected to an Arduino. The Arduino's information can then be transferred to the EV3 Intelligent Brick by an I2C connection. An EV3 motor can serve as a platform for scanning the lidar beam in either azimuth or elevation, with control of both the motor and the lidar under an EV3 program. A camera is a useful addition to the lidar, combining distance information with imagery from the camera. This camera can be implemented with a LEGO-compatible device with the Vision Subsystem v5 made by Mindsensors.com.

CHAPTER 9

The LEGO Weather Station—SPI Sensor with EV3 I2C Interface

Another sensor interface often encountered is the serial peripheral interface (SPI), which will be worked with in this chapter. SPI will be used to transfer commands and data between the sensor and the Arduino. I2C is brought in to transfer data to the EV3 Intelligent Brick. So, two interfaces are used in the project described in this chapter: SPI and I2C. The I2C setup is similar to that used in Chapter 8, so the emphasis will be on SPI in this chapter. The project involved is to build a weather monitoring sensor, using the EV3 Intelligent Brick as a display and data logger. An EV3 Color Sensor is also part of the system to record ambient light levels. Weather measurements are made with the SparkFun Atmospheric Sensor (`www.sparkfun.com`), shown in Figure 9-1, which provides data on temperature, humidity, and barometric pressure. These measurements, along with ambient light level from the EV3 Color Sensor, will be displayed on the EV3 Intelligent Brick and stored in a file that can be downloaded for study of weather variables over time.

© Grady Koch 2020
G. Koch, *The LEGO Arduino Cookbook*, https://doi.org/10.1007/978-1-4842-6303-7_9

Figure 9-1. *The SparkFun Atmospheric Sensor provides measurements of temperature, pressure, and barometric pressure*

Mounting the Atmospheric Sensor

The Atmospheric Sensor takes atmospheric readings from a small chip on the sensor's circuit board, so this chip should have exposure to as much of the air around it as possible. This exposure can be facilitated by having the chip facing upward, with minimal structure around the device. The Atmospheric Sensor has solder pads on its circuit board for electronic connections, which could be used for soldering in wires. But a header soldered in place allows for a tidier implementation, as has been done in Figure 9-2.

Figure 9-2. *A header installed on the underside of the circuit board helps to keep the sensing area on the top of the board clear of structures that might affect air flow around the sensor*

Building the LEGO Weather Station

Figure 9-3 shows a mounting design, using an M3 screw to hold one of the circuit board's corner holes to a Technic open center frame liftarm. A nut placed under the liftarm keeps the Atmospheric Sensor in place. The other side of the liftarm serves as an attachment point for the EV3 Color Sensor. Building instructions for this design can be found in the following.

Figure 9-3. *Sensors are held on a Technic liftarm for the LEGO Weather Station*

x1
3701
1 x 4 Technic Brick with Holes

x1
2730
1 x 10 Technic Brick with Holes

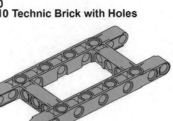

x1
64178
5 x 11 Open Center Frame Liftarm

x1
95650
EV3 Color Sensor

x2
6558
Long Technic Pin with Friction Ridges

x2
2780
Technic Pin with Friction Ridges

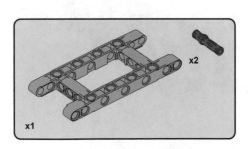

1

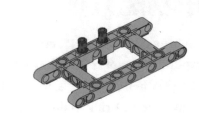

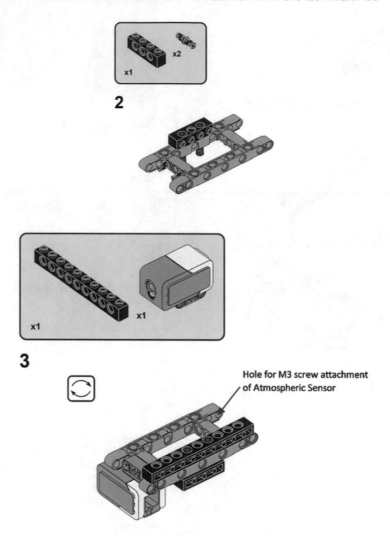

Hole for M3 screw attachment
of Atmospheric Sensor

Wiring Connections

There are four sets of wiring connections to make for the LEGO Weather
Station: (1) the Atmospheric Sensor to Arduino, (2) the Arduino to
Breadboard Connector, (3) the EV3 Color Sensor to EV3 Intelligent
Brick, and (4) the EV3 Intelligent Brick to Breadboard Connector.

The Atmospheric Sensor to Arduino connection is made by jumper wires, as diagrammed in Figure 9-4. Jumper wires are also used in the second set of wiring connections, as in Figure 9-5, for the communication between the Arduino and the EV3 Intelligent Brick. Finally, EV3 Connector Cables link the EV3 Intelligent Brick to both a Breadboard Connector and an EV3 Color Sensor, diagrammed in Figure 9-6.

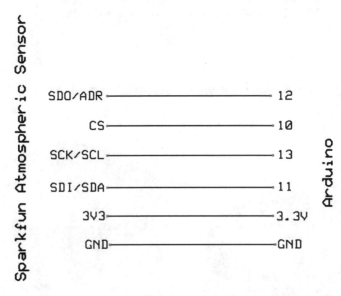

Figure 9-4. *Connection between the SparkFun Atmospheric Sensor and the Arduino is by six jumper wires*

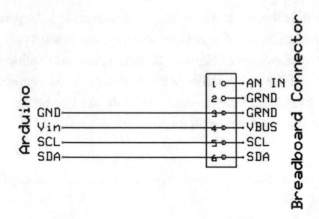

Figure 9-5. *Connection between the Arduino and the EV3 Intelligent Brick is by I2C*

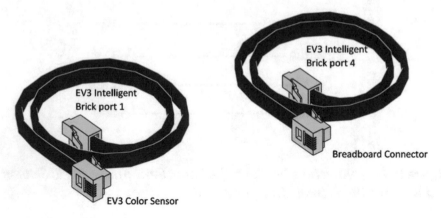

Figure 9-6. *EV3 Connector Cables get plugged into ports 1 and 4 on the EV3 Intelligent Brick*

EV3 Code

The purpose of the EV3 program for the LEGO Weather Station is to read in measurements from the SparkFun Atmospheric Sensor on temperature, humidity, and barometric pressure. In addition, a measurement of the ambient light level is taken from an EV3 Color Sensor. These four measurements are displayed on the front panel of the EV3 Intelligent Brick and stored in a log of data. The data log can be downloaded from the EV3 Intelligent Brick for further processing and analysis. Figure 9-7 shows the EV3 program for these tasks.

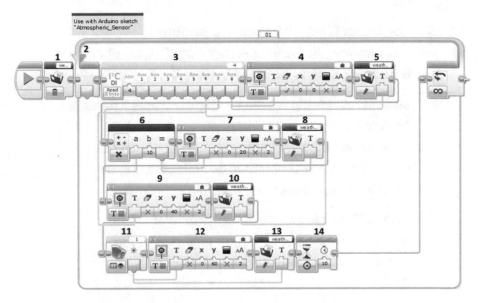

Figure 9-7. *EV3 code for the LEGO Weather Station works with I2C data passed on port 4 and an EV3 Color Sensor on port 1*

Steps in the EV3 code include

1. File Access Block: Clears memory on the EV3 Intelligent Brick of a file under the name weather log.

2. Loop Block: Sets up an infinite repetition of taking in measurements to display and store.

3. I2C Block: Reads 3 bytes of data over the I2C link connected to port 4. The remaining 5 bytes of data are not used in this project.

4. Display Block: Prints the results of I2C byte 8 on the front panel display of the EV3 Intelligent Brick, corresponding to temperature. Units of Fahrenheit for temperature are used, as set up in the Arduino sketch.

5. File Access Block: Stores the temperature measurement in the file weather log. This number is the same as that displayed in block 4.

6. Math Block: Multiplies the results of I2C byte 7 times 10. Byte 7 is a measurement of pressure, which is scaled down in the Arduino sketch to fit within the range of 7-bit representation. So multiplication by 10 in this block compensates for the adjustment.

7. Display Block: Prints the measurement of barometric pressure, in units of millibars, as the second row on the display of the EV3 Intelligent Brick.

8. File Access Block: Stores the pressure measurement into the weather log data file.

9. Display Block: Prints the results of I2C byte 6 on the front panel display of the EV3 Intelligent Brick, corresponding to relative humidity. Units of this measurement are percent.

10. File Access Block: Stores the relative humidity into the weather log data file.

11. Color Sensor Block: Measures the ambient light intensity.

12.   Display Block: Prints the ambient light intensity measurement on the fourth line of the EV3 Intelligent Brick front panel. Units of this measurement are on a scale of 0 to 100, with 0 being complete darkness and 100 being very bright.

13.   File Access Block: Stores the ambient light intensity into the weather log data file.

14.   Wait Block: Delays action by 10 seconds. In other words, the four recorded weather variables are repeated every 10 seconds.

Arduino Sketch

The Arduino sketch, shown in Listing 9-1, sets up an interface over an SPI link to the Atmospheric Sensor, bringing in the measurement of temperature, pressure, and humidity. These variables are then passed to the EV3 Intelligent Brick using an I2C link, similar to the I2C design used in Chapter 8.

Listing 9-1.   The Arduino sketch for using the SparkFun Atmospheric Sensor should be run at the same time as the EV3 program "weather_station"

```
/*--------------------------------------------------
  LEGO Weather Station

  This script reads temperature, pressure, and humidity from
  the SparkFun Electronics Atmospheric Sensor (based on a
  BME280)
```

```
Connections:
Atmospheric Sensor GND to Arduino GND
Atmospheric Sensor 3V3 to Arduino 3.3V
Atmospheric Sensor CS to Arduino Pin 10
Atmospheric Sensor SDI/SDA to Arduino Pin 11
Atmospheric Sensor SDO/ADR to Arduino Pin 12
Atmospheric Sensor SCK/SCL to Arduino Pin 13
EV3 Breadboard VBUS to Arduino VIN
EV3 Breadboard GRND (next to VBUS) to Arduino GND
EV3 Breadboard SCL to Arduino SCL
EV3 Breadboard SDA to Arduino SDA
EV3 cable between Breadboard Connector and Port 4 of EV3
Intelligent Brick
EV3 cable between EV3 Color Sensor and Port 1 of EV3
Intelligent Brick

Use with EV3 program "weather_station"

Sections of code taken from SparkFun Electronics github site,
written by Nathan Seidle

Arduino to EV3 connection modified from Dexter Industries post
www.dexterindustries.com/howto/connecting-ev3-arduino

----------------------------------------------------*/

#include <SPI.h>  //Call library for SPI communication
#include "SparkFunBME280.h"  //Call library for BME280 sensor
#include <Wire.h>  //Call library for I2C communication

#define SLAVE_ADDRESS 0x04  //I2C address for communicating
with EV3 Intelligent
//Brick.  Same address should be in EV3 program

BME280 mySensor;
```

```
byte c[]={10,11,12,13,14,15,16,17}; //Declare array that will
                                be sent to EV3
//Intelligent Brick.  Load with dummy variables that can help
de-bugging

void setup()
{
  Serial.begin(9600);  //Start serial communications.  Serial
                    monitor must match this baud rate.
  Wire.begin(SLAVE_ADDRESS); //Start I2C link
  Serial.println("Reading basic values from BME280");

  if (mySensor.beginSPI(10) == false) //Begin communication over
                                SPI. Use pin 10 as CS.
  {
    Serial.println("The sensor did not respond. Please check
    wiring.");
    while(1); //Freeze
  }
}

void loop()
{
  Serial.print(" Temp= ");  //Print label on serial monitor for
                        diagnostic purposes
  Serial.print(mySensor.readTempF(), 2);  //Print for
                                    diagnostic purposes
  c[0] = round(mySensor.readTempF());  //Load value into array
                                to be sent to EV3

  Serial.print(" Pressure= ");  //Print label on serial monitor
                        for diagnostic purposes
```

```
  Serial.print(mySensor.readFloatPressure(), 0); //Print for
                                      diagnostic
                                      purposes
  c[1] = round(mySensor.readFloatPressure()/1000); //Load value
                                      into array
                                      to be sent
                                      to EV3

  Serial.print(" Humidity= "); //Print label on serial monitor
                      for diagnostic purposes
  Serial.print(mySensor.readFloatHumidity(), 0); //Print for
                                      diagnostic
                                      purposes
  c[2] = round(mySensor.readFloatHumidity()); //Load value into
                                      array to be sent
                                      to EV3

  Serial.println();

  Wire.onRequest(sendData); //Send data to EV3

  delay(100);
}

//Function for sending data.
void sendData()
{
  Wire.write(c,8); //c is the array of 8 bytes length
}
```

Example Application: Diurnal Weather Trends

Temperature and humidity typically cycle through a pattern over the course of a day, which can be studied with the LEGO Weather Station by letting it run for a day or longer. Battery lifetime becomes an issue for such an experiment, with alkaline batteries lasting for about 10 hours when powering the LEGO Weather Station. So in the following experiment, measurements were occasionally interrupted to download data and change out batteries. Data, in the form of the file weather log, can be downloaded from the EV3 Intelligent Brick in the EV3 programming environment by selecting Tools ➤ Memory Browser from the toolbar. A menu will then appear to select the file of interest, weather log in this case.

Opening weather log with a text editor shows a long list of numbers, such as in Figure 9-8. These numbers are a group of temperature, pressure, humidity, and ambient light, repeated and recorded every ten seconds. To investigate diurnal weather trends, the data of temperature, humidity, and ambient light are of interest, so they have been brought into a spreadsheet program. As an example, Figure 9-9 shows a graph of temperature and ambient light, and Figure 9-10 shows a graph of humidity and ambient light. Several features are of note:

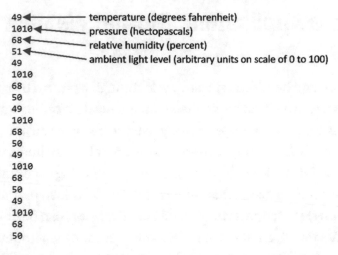

Figure 9-8. *Opening the weather log should show a long list of numbers consisting of temperature, pressure, humidity, and ambient light measurements repeated every 10 seconds*

- Ambient light level, which is plotted in both Figures 9-9 and 9-10, changes with night and day, and transitions of sunrises and sunsets are easily identified. Variation is seen in the ambient light level in the hours after sunrise as shadows came across the face of the sensor. The LEGO Weather Station was placed in an area with trees that morning sunlight passes through, creating shadows through the branches and leaves of trees.

- The temperature plot of Figure 9-9 shows temperature rising after sunrise and falling after sunset, as is expected. A maximum temperature was seen in this 2.3-day-long data set of 72F, and a minimum was 35F. The LEGO Weather Station functioned without problems in cold temperatures. Some spikes in temperature were seen in the morning hours that are related to direct sunlight warming the LEGO Weather Station.

- The humidity plot of Figure 9-10 shows a pattern of relative humidity falling during the day and rising at night. Relative humidity is related to temperature, so a correlation is seen between the trends of temperature going up and relative humidity going down. High humidity at night combined with lower temperature often results in early morning dew formation.

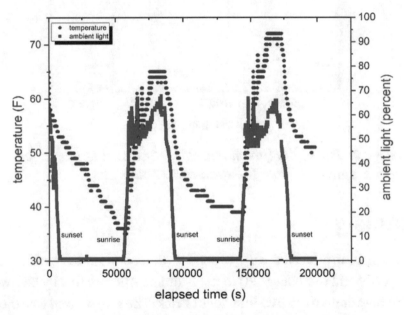

Figure 9-9. *Temperature (red circles) and ambient light level (blue squares) are graphed over the span of 55 hours*

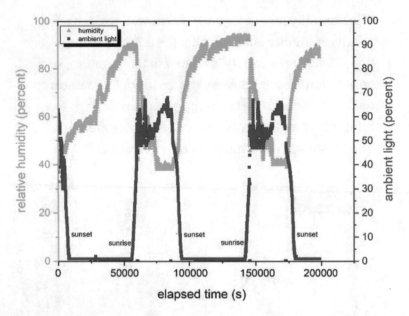

Figure 9-10. *Humidity (green triangles) and ambient light level (blue squares) are graphed over the span of 55 hours*

Summary

This chapter introduced the use of sensors that communicate with the serial peripheral interface (SPI) to the Arduino. Another link by I2C was used to pass data to the EV3 Intelligent Brick. The sensor used was the SparkFun Atmospheric Sensor to build a weather monitoring instrument of temperature, pressure, and humidity. In addition, the EV3 Color Sensor was employed to measure ambient light intensity. These four weather parameters were displayed and recorded on the EV3 Intelligent Brick, showing the function of the EV3 Intelligent Brick as a data logger. Weather data stored on the EV3 Intelligent Brick was downloaded to show how weather variables change over the course of a day.

CHAPTER 10

The LEGO Spectrum Analyzer—Arduino Shield with I2C Output to EV3

The sensors used in this book so far have been components that plug into the Arduino board with jumper wire connections. But there are many sensors and controllers that attach onto the Arduino board, called *shields*, such that they lay up against the Arduino board. Electronic and power connections are made to a shield by the headers on the Arduino board. The use of shields is introduced in this chapter, including incorporation into LEGO projects. The example project is a Spectrum Shield shown in Figure 10-1, made by SparkFun (`www.sparkfun.com`), that analyzes an audio signal's spectral content. The input audio signal is separated into seven frequency bands and analyzed for power within each spectral band. In this project, an EV3 Intelligent Brick will use the spectral information to graphically represent audio content on an LED array and make LEGO mechanisms dance in time to music.

© Grady Koch 2020
G. Koch, *The LEGO Arduino Cookbook*, https://doi.org/10.1007/978-1-4842-6303-7_10

Figure 10-1.   *The Spectrum Shield analyzes audio input for content in seven frequency bands*

Mounting the Spectrum Shield

Many Arduino shields, including the Spectrum Shield, come from the manufacturer without headers installed. The headers to be installed may have to be ordered separately from the shield, as is the case with the Spectrum Shield. The set of headers is shown in Figure 10-2, with one of the four headers soldered into place. After all four headers have been installed, the shield is pressed into place on the STEMTera, as in Figure 10-3.

Figure 10-2. *Headers for the Spectrum Shield need to be soldered in place*

Figure 10-3. *The Spectrum Shield is installed with header pins lining up with the sockets on the STEMTera*

Building the Spectral Display

To create an interesting display of audio spectrum information, two approaches can be taken, both implemented in Figure 10-4. One approach is to show each frequency's power content as a vertical bar on an LED Matrix made by Mindsensors.com. This matrix display has been built to be LEGO compatible, including an EV3 programming block.

The second approach to the spectral display is to connect a motor to one or more of the spectral channels, with the power applied to the motor proportional to the power in the spectral channel. Various motions can be connected to the motor to create, for example, flapping, clapping, and up-and-down motions. These three motions are used in Figure 10-4, using mechanism designs adapted from Yoshihito Isogawa's *The LEGO MINDSTORMS EV3 Idea Book*. With their motions linked to audio input, the mechanisms appear to be dancing when music is input.

Figure 10-4. *An LED Matrix and three motorized mechanisms have been attached to the LEGO Arduino Workstation*

Wiring Connections

The shield's headers take care of the wiring connections between the Arduino and sensor in this project, so there is no cable involved. The remaining connection that does involve wiring is between the Arduino and the EV3 Intelligent Brick. I2C communication will be used to send measurement results to the EV3 Intelligent Brick, involving the wiring connection shown in Figure 10-5. Finally, there are five EV3 cables to connect, as diagrammed in Figure 10-6. Three of these EV3 cable connections are to motors, one is to the Breadboard Connector, and one is from the Mindsensors.com LED Matrix.

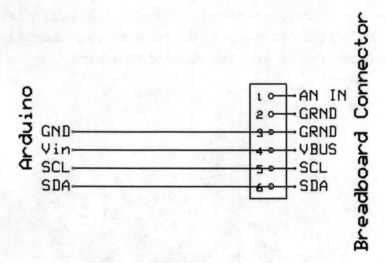

Figure 10-5. *Communication between the Arduino and the EV3 Intelligent Brick is by I2C*

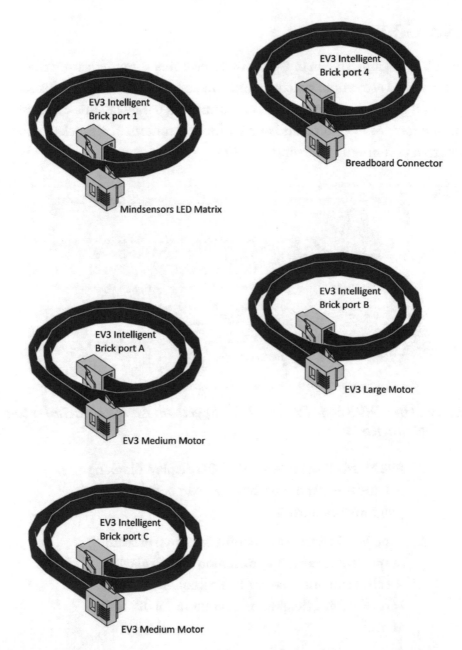

Figure 10-6. *EV3 Connector Cables are plugged into ports 1, 4, A, B, and C on the EV3 Intelligent Brick*

EV3 Code

The EV3 program, shown in Figure 10-7, takes measurements from the Arduino and uses audio spectrum information to drive an LED Matrix and a set of EV3 motors. Two routines are running in parallel in this code, one routine for the LED Matrix and one for the EV3 motors. The blocks in this program perform the following functions:

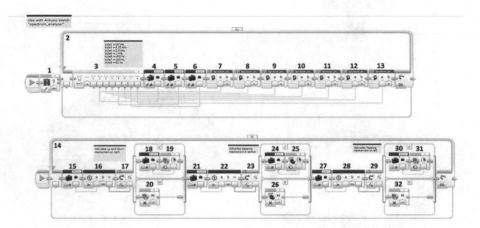

Figure 10-7. *EV3 code for the LEGO Spectrum Analyzer includes two parallel programs*

1. EV3 Matrix Block: Clears the LED display, blanking out any pixels that may have been lit before the program was started.

2. Loop Block: Executes a continuous loop of reading in spectrum analysis information and displaying spectral content in seven audio frequency bands as bars of varying height on the columns of the LED Matrix.

3. I2C Block: Reads 8 bytes of data from the Arduino over the I2C connection on port 4 of the EV3 Intelligent Brick. Byte 1 on this block is not used, since the Spectrum Shield only analyzes seven frequency bands.

4. Variable Block: Loads the I2C reading for byte 2 into a variable called byte2. This variable will be read by the program running in parallel that starts in block 14.

5. Variable Block: Loads the I2C reading for byte 5 into a variable called byte5.

6. Variable Block: Loads the I2C reading for byte 7 into a variable called byte7.

7. Spectrum_Analyzer My Block: Displays the value of byte 2 in column 0 of the LED Matrix. The code for this My Block is shown in Figure 10-8.

8. Spectrum_Analyzer My Block: Displays the value of byte 3 in column 1 of the LED Matrix.

9. Spectrum_Analyzer My Block: Displays the value of byte 4 in column 2 of the LED Matrix.

10. Spectrum_Analyzer My Block: Displays the value of byte 5 in column 3 of the LED Matrix.

11. Spectrum_Analyzer My Block: Displays the value of byte 6 in column 4 of the LED Matrix.

12. Spectrum_Analyzer My Block: Displays the value of byte 7 in column 5 of the LED Matrix.

13. Spectrum_Analyzer My Block: Displays the value of byte 8 in column 6 of the LED Matrix.

14. Loop Block: Begins the other routine running in parallel with the preceding tasks. This second infinite loop sends signals to activate three motors with a power proportional to the signal content in three audio frequency bands. The mechanisms connected to these motors appear to dance in time to music input to the Spectrum Shield. The three frequency bands selected are in bass, midrange, and treble parts of the spectrum as frequencies centered at 160 Hz, 1 kHz, and 16 kHz.

15. Variable Block: Recalls the value stored in variable byte2.

16. Compare Block: Checks if the value in byte2 is above a noise threshold. The noise threshold value is set for 20 in this block. Even when no audio signal is given to the Spectrum Shield, it was found that a level of about 10 was constant as noise background. So only signals above this noise floor are considered in driving the motor dancing mechanisms.

17. Switch Block: Presents true and false paths corresponding to whether byte2 is above the noise threshold.

18. Variable Block: Begins the Switch true path by recalling the value stored in variable byte2.

19. Medium Motor Block: Spins the Medium Motor connection to port C with power stored in byte2. So for louder audio input, the motor will spin faster.

20. Medium Motor Block: Takes the false path of the
     Switch block to turn off the motor connected to port
     C. This action is taken when there is no spectrum
     signal in byte2.

21–26. Repeat blocks 15 to 20, but for spectral content
        contained in byte5 that drives a Large Motor
        connected to port B of the EV3 Intelligent Brick.
        byte5 contains spectral information on the audio
        midrange band of frequencies, centered at 1 kHz.

27–32. Repeat blocks 15 to 20, but for spectral content
        contained in byte7 that drives a Medium Motor
        connected to port A of the EV3 Intelligent Brick.
        byte7 contains spectral information on the audio
        bass band of frequencies, centered at 160 Hz.

The program of Figure 10-7 makes use of a My Block, shown in
Figure 10-8, called spectrum_analyzer, which translates the level of a
signal measured in a frequency range into a bar of LEDs lit up in a column
of the LED Matrix. The height of this bar corresponds to the strength of the
signal.

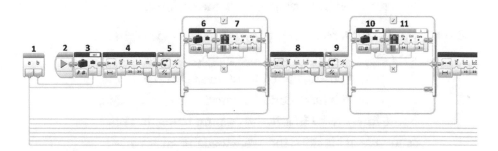

Figure 10-8. *The* spectrum_analyzer *My Block assigns column
values to the LED Matrix*

Steps in this My Block include

1. Parameters: Defines two parameters used in the program—a for the spectral value being tested and b for the column of the LED Matrix.

2. Start Block: Declares the beginning of the programming steps.

3. Variable Block: Writes the column parameter as a variable called col.

4. Range Block: Tests the spectral value parameter for being within a range of, in this case, 20 to 30. A true/false logic value is output from this block.

5. Switch Block: Executes blocks 6–7 if the Range block has a true output. Otherwise, no action is taken.

6. Variable Block: Recalls the value in the col variable to indicate a column number.

7. EV3 Matrix Block: Displays the value of 1 in column 0. The column value number is represented in binary representation l. Hence, the value of 1 written here turns on the lowest LED in the column.

8–11. Duplicate blocks 4–7, but testing for the next higher level of the spectral value. If the spectral value is in the range of 30–40, then the column is lit up with the value of 3. In binary-coded decimal, 3 is represented by the lower two LEDs in the column being lit. This sequence of blocks is then repeated for values of 40–50, 50–60, 60–70, 70–80, 90–100, and > 100 with corresponding LED values of 7, 15, 31, 63, 127, and 255. These additional six sets of blocks are not shown in Figure 10-8 in order to fit the figure on the page.

Arduino Sketch

The Arduino sketch, given in Listing 10-1, reads data from the Spectrum Shield, resulting in an array of seven values that indicates the power level in seven spectral bands. These spectral bands are centered at frequency values of 63 Hz, 160 Hz, 400 Hz, 1 kHz, 2.5 kHz, 6.25 kHz, and 16 kHz. The values passed along by the Arduino sketch indicate the amount of power within each frequency band, using I2C transfer to send data to the EV3 Intelligent Brick. The I2C transfer between the Arduino and the EV3 is set up for moving 8 bytes of data, so with only 7 bytes of interest, the remaining byte is loaded with a dummy variable.

Listing 10-1. The Arduino sketch for using the Spectrum Shield should be run at the same time as the EV3 program "analyzer_with_ motors"

```
/*----------------------------------------------------
LEGO Spectrum Analyzer
Takes audio spectrum analysis from SparkFun Spectrum shield
to display spectral content on LED Matrix and trigger three
motorized mechanism.
Data is passed from the Arduino to EV3 Intelligent Brick by I2C
connection.

Connections:
EV3 Breadboard Connector VBUS to Arduino VIN
EV3 Breadboard Connector GRND (next to VBUS) to Arduino GND
EV3 Breadboard Connector SCL to Arduino SCL
EV3 Breadboard Connector SDA to Arduino SDA
EV3 cable between Breadboard Connector and Port 4 of EV3
Intelligent Brick
Mindsensors LED Matrix to Port 1 of EV3 Intelligent Brick
```

EV3 cable between EV3 Medium Motor and Port A of EV3 Intelligent Brick
EV3 cable between EV3 Large Motor and Port B of EV3 Intelligent Brick
EV3 cable between EV3 Medium Motor and Port C of EV3 Intelligent Brick
1/8 inch audio plug between audio source and Spectrum Shield Input
1/8 inch audio plug between external speark and Spectrum Shield Output

This script is used in conjunction with EV3 code "analyzer_with_motors".

Sections of code below were originally developed by Toni Klopfenstein of SparkFun Electronics and Ben Moyes of Bliptronnics.
Original code and other examples can be found at https://github.com/sparkfun/Spectrum_Shield

Arduino to EV3 connection modified from Dexter Industries post www.dexterindustries.com/howto/connecting-ev3-arduino.

```
-----------------------------------------------------*/

//Declare Spectrum Shield pin connections
#define STROBE 4
#define RESET 6
#define DC_One A0
#define DC_Two A1

#include <Wire.h>  //Call library for I2C communication
```

```
#define SLAVE_ADDRESS 0x04  //I2C address for communicating
with EV3 Intelligent Brick.
//Same address should be in EV3 program.

byte c[]={10,11,12,13,14,15,16,17};   //Declare array that will
                                     be sent to EV3
//Intelligent Brick.  Load with dummy values that can help
de-bugging

//Define spectrum variables
int freq_amp;
int Frequencies_One[7];
int Frequencies_Two[7];
int i;

void setup() {

  Serial.begin(9600);  //Start serial communication.  Serial
                     monitor must match this baud rate.

  //Set Spectrum Shield pin configurations
  pinMode(STROBE, OUTPUT);
  pinMode(RESET, OUTPUT);
  pinMode(DC_One, INPUT);
  pinMode(DC_Two, INPUT);
  digitalWrite(STROBE, HIGH);
  digitalWrite(RESET, HIGH);

  //Initialize Spectrum Analyzers
  digitalWrite(STROBE, LOW);
  delay(1);
  digitalWrite(RESET, HIGH);
  delay(1);
  digitalWrite(STROBE, HIGH);
```

```
  delay(1);
  digitalWrite(STROBE, LOW);
  delay(1);
  digitalWrite(RESET, LOW);

  Wire.begin(SLAVE_ADDRESS);

}

void loop() {

  Read_Frequencies();

  Serial.println(Frequencies_One[0]); //Serial output is used
                                      as a diagnostic.
  //Fill 8 bytes that will be sent to EV3 Intelligent Brick.
  //Values are divided by 10 to fit within 8-bit word.
  //Only seven spectral bands are reported by Spectrum Shield,
  //so c[7] is loaded with a dummy value.
  c[0] = Frequencies_One[0]/10;
  c[1] = Frequencies_One[1]/10;
  c[2] = Frequencies_One[2]/10;
  c[3] = Frequencies_One[3]/10;
  c[4] = Frequencies_One[4]/10;
  c[5] = Frequencies_One[5]/10;
  c[6] = Frequencies_One[6]/10;
  c[7] = 0;

  Wire.onRequest(sendData); //Send data to EV3

  delay(50);
```

```
}

//Function for sending data
void sendData()
{
  Wire.write(c,8); // c is the array of 8 bytes length.
}

//Function for reading frequencies from Spectrum Shield
void Read_Frequencies(){
  //Read frequencies for each band
  for (freq_amp = 0; freq_amp<7; freq_amp++)
  {
    Frequencies_One[freq_amp] = analogRead(DC_One);
    Frequencies_Two[freq_amp] = analogRead(DC_Two);
    digitalWrite(STROBE, HIGH);
    digitalWrite(STROBE, LOW);
  }
}
```

Results

To use the LEGO Spectrum Analyzer, an audio signal is plugged into the Input jack on the Spectrum Shield. The audio signal can also be listened to by plugging an amplified speaker into the Output jack of the Spectrum Shield. Video examples of the results can be seen on www.hightechlego. com, with test cases of a digital drum kit, acoustic guitar, and iPhone audio sources. In these examples, matching the EV3 code and the Arduino sketch earlier, the spectra centered at 160 Hz, 1 kHz, and 16 kHz are connected to motors to animate mechanisms. These spectra can, of course, be changed with modification to the EV3 code. While a lower bass frequency of 63 Hz is available as an output of the Spectrum Shield, it is not a very active frequency in most music. Hence, 160 Hz was used to represent the low-frequency end in the example videos. Drum and percussion instruments have the most varied spectral content, often triggering the low- and high-frequency ends of the spectrum. Guitar sounds, in contrast, are in the midrange of spectrum, so the high- and low-frequency mechanisms seldom get triggered.

Summary

This chapter explored the use of shields with the Arduino. Shields can offer more complex functions than a stand-alone sensor or controller, as was seen with the example project of a Spectrum Shield. This Spectrum Shield analyzes an audio signal for spectral content, such that power within separate spectral bands can be used to manipulate displays or motorized actions. In the example project, audio spectrum information was displayed in two ways: on an LED matrix to create a bar graph of spectral information and with motorized mechanisms that move in time to music. In the next chapter, another use of a shield will be described for moving data in the opposite direction from the design in this chapter, to move sensor data from the EV3 Intelligent Brick to the shield.

CHAPTER 11

Favorite Color Machine—Arduino Shield with I2C Output from EV3

The I2C projects of the previous chapters had the Arduino hosting a sensor to pass data to the EV3 Intelligent Brick. In this chapter, the reverse arrangement is presented of using the EV3 Intelligent Brick as a sensor host to pass data to the Arduino. The project involved here is to have a user-selected color displayed on an LED array shield attached to the Arduino. The user can adjust the level of each of the three component colors of red, green, and blue to dial in any color. The LED array is in the form of the Adafruit NeoPixel Shield (`www.adafruit.com`), pictured in Figure 11-1. Sensor input is by the rotation of adjustment knobs, using the rotation sensing function of EV3 Medium Motors. Three such motors are involved, one for each of the three constituent colors.

© Grady Koch 2020
G. Koch, *The LEGO Arduino Cookbook*, https://doi.org/10.1007/978-1-4842-6303-7_11

Figure 11-1. *The Adafruit NeoPixel Shield features a rectangular array of 40 color-programmable LEDs*

Mounting the NeoPixel Shield

The NeoPixel Shield comes delivered without headers installed, but headers are supplied for applications that prefer the use of headers. So these headers need to be soldered onto the NeoPixel Shield circuit board. With headers installed, the shield can be pressed into place on the Arduino, as shown in Figure 11-2. Each of the LEDs on the NeoPixel Shield can be addressed individually to turn on any or all of the elements in the array in any desired color. In the arrangement of Figure 11-1, LED number 1 is the upper-left corner. For the Favorite Color Machine built in this chapter, all of LEDs in the array will be programmed for the same color.

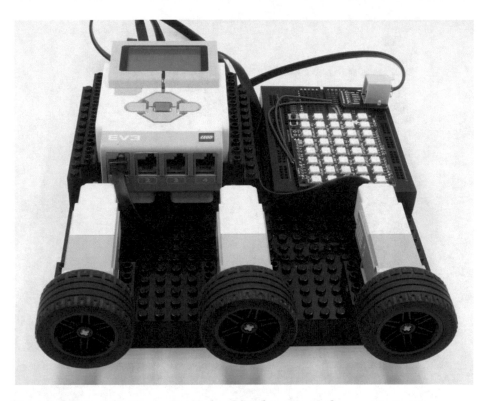

Figure 11-2. *The Favorite Color Machine uses three rotation sensors to adjust the color of a NeoPixel Shield*

Mounting the LEGO Motors

An EV3 Medium Motor, aside from its obvious function as a motor, can be used as a rotation sensor. With an axle connected to the motor shaft, rotating the axle by hand creates a signal indicating the number of degrees that the shaft has been rotated. This functionality can make an adjustment knob out of an EV3 Medium Motor—three such adjustment knobs are used to build the Favorite Color Machine, as shown in Figure 11-2. Building instructions for a mount design for the EV3 Medium Motor are presented as follows.

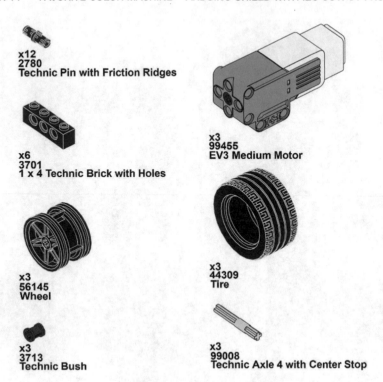

x12
2780
Technic Pin with Friction Ridges

x6
3701
1 x 4 Technic Brick with Holes

x3
56145
Wheel

x3
3713
Technic Bush

x3
99455
EV3 Medium Motor

x3
44309
Tire

x3
99008
Technic Axle 4 with Center Stop

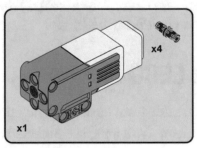

x4

x1

1

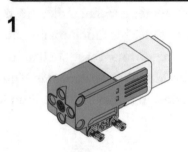

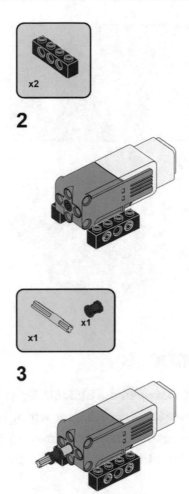

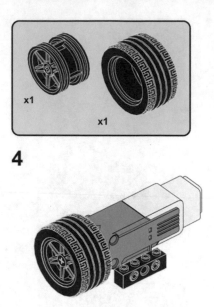

Wiring Connections

Data transfer is over I2C between the EV3 Intelligent Brick and the Arduino via the Breadboard Connector, involving the wiring in the schematic of Figure 11-3. The second set of connections involves EV3 Connector Cables, diagrammed in Figure 11-4, to the Breadboard Connector and EV3 motors.

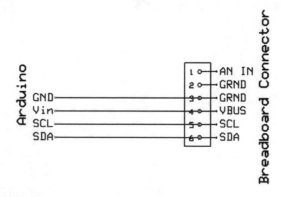

Figure 11-3. *Communication between the Arduino and the EV3 Intelligent Brick is by I2C*

Figure 11-4. *Connector Cables link to three EV3 Medium Motors and the Breadboard Connector*

EV3 Code

The EV3 program is developed in the following in two parts. The first part, to be made into a My Block for each of the three constituent colors, reads if the adjustment knobs are being turned and, if so, increments a value representative of the level of the three constituent colors. Three such My Blocks are made, one for each color, and then used in an EV3 program for displaying constituent color levels and sending data to the Arduino. The My Block program for reading knob adjustments and setting a variable indicating a color level is shown in Figure 11-5. This set of code blocks is for the red level of adjustment—My Blocks of identical commands need to be made for green and blue colors. The differences among the My Blocks are in the variable name (red, green, or blue) and the port to which the EV3 Medium Motor is connected (red for port A, green for port B, and blue for port C). Steps in the program include

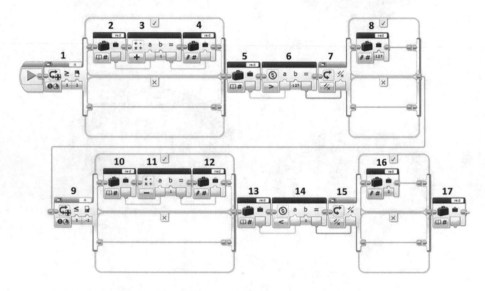

Figure 11-5. *EV3 code to form a My Block that determines the level of red based on the rotation input from the EV3 Medium Motor*

1. Switch Block: Presents true and false path options, based on whether the EV3 Medium Motor connected to port A is rotated clockwise.

2. Variable Block: Begins the true path of the Switch block by reading the current value of the variable called red. This variable will be initialized in the EV3 program that calls this My Block.

3. Math Block: Adds 1 to the value of the red variable.

4. Variable Block: Stores the new value of the red variable.

5. Variable Block: Reads the new, updated value of the red variable.

6. Compare Block: Checks if the red value is greater than 127 and, if so, creates a true flag as output. As described in Chapter 7, only a value of up to 127 can be passed by the I2C block that will be used later.

7. Switch Block: Creates true and false paths based on the input from the Compare block.

8. Variable Block: Reassigns the value of red to 127, in the event that the Compare block found red to be greater than 127. In other words, the value of red is capped at 127.

9–12. Sense if motor rotation input is counterclockwise, as opposed to the clockwise case of blocks 1–4. For counterclockwise rotation, the value of red is decreased, rather than increased.

13–16. Test if the value of red has decreased to below 0, and if so, reassign the value to be 0.

17. Variable Block: Reads the value of the red variable. This step creates an output when a My Block is created.

The My Blocks for representing each color can then be used in the program of Figure 11-6, taking input for each of the three motors to set a level for the red, green, and blue constituent colors. These color values are sent to the Arduino over I2C, as well as displayed on the EV3 Intelligent Brick's front panel.

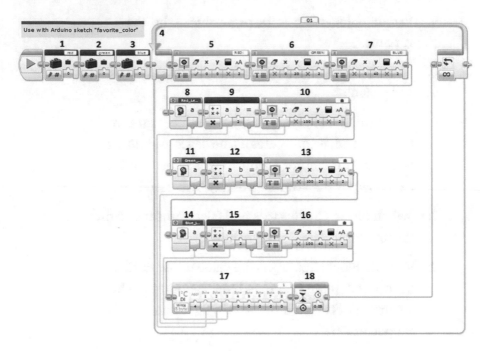

Figure 11-6. *My Blocks, such as the one created in Figure 11-5, read rotational movement of motors to represent color values*

Specific programming blocks include

1–3.   Variable Blocks: Initialize variables called red, green, and blue and set their values to 0. These values will be updated as the rest of the program executes.

4.   Loop Block: Sets up an infinite repetition of reading color values to display and send to the Arduino.

5–7.   Display Blocks: Create labels on the front panel of the EV3 Intelligent Brick to identify the values that will be printed on the screen in later steps.

8.   Red_Level My Block: Sets a level for the red constituent color as assigned by manual rotation of an EV3 Medium Motor. This My Block was programmed in Figure 11-5.

9. Math Block: Multiplies the output from the Red_Level My Block by 2 to account for the 7-bit maximum level of 127 that can be passed by I2C. As will be seen in the Arduino code of the following section, a multiplication by 2 also takes place before color levels are sent to the NeoPixel Shield. The NeoPixel Shield accepts a value represented by 8 bits to a maximum value of 255.

10. Display Block: Prints the red level color assignment on the front panel of the EV3 Intelligent Brick. This value will be displayed next to the label created in block 5.

11–13. Repeat the steps of blocks 8–10 for the green level color assignment.

14–16. Repeat the steps of blocks 8–10 for the blue level color assignment.

17. I2C Block: Writes 3 bytes of data to the Arduino, with 1 byte each representing the constituent color values of red, green, and blue.

18. Wait Block: Pauses the program to avoid an overflow of data being passed to the Arduino.

Arduino Sketch

The Arduino sketch, given in Listing 11-1, reads 3 bytes over I2C as written by the EV3 Intelligent Brick. Each of these bytes represents a color level then sent to the NeoPixel Shield.

Listing 11-1. The Arduino sketch for using the NeoPixel Shield should be run at the same time as the EV3 program "favorite_color"

```
/*------------------------------------------------------
Favorite Color Machine

  This script sets the color of an Adafruit NeoPixel Array
  based on red/green/blue input from the EV3 Intelligent
  Brick. Each red/green/blue component setting is generated
  by the EV3 Intelligent Brick and passed over I2C to the Arduino

  Connections:
  EV3 Breadboard VBUS to Arduino VIN
  EV3 Breadboard GRND (next to VBUS) to Arduino GND
  EV3 Breadboard SCL to Arduino SCL
  EV3 Breadboard SDA to Arduino SDA
  EV3 cable between breadboard connector and Port 1 of EV3
  Intelligent Brick

  Use with EV3 program "favorite color.ev3"

  Arduino to EV3 connection modified from Dexter Industries post
  www.dexterindustries.com/howto/connecting-ev3-arduino

  ------------------------------------------------------*/

#include <Adafruit_NeoPixel.h>
#include <Wire.h>  //Call library for I2C communications

#define SLAVE_ADDRESS 0x04  //I2C address for communicating
with EV3 Intelligent
//Brick.  Same address should be in EV3 program

const int ROWS = 5;
const int COLS = 8;
```

```
const int NUM_LEDS = ROWS * COLS;
const int LED_PIN = 6;
Adafruit_NeoPixel strip = Adafruit_NeoPixel(NUM_LEDS, LED_PIN,
NEO_GRB + NEO_KHZ800);

void setup()
{
    strip.begin();
    strip.show(); //Initialize all pixels to 'off'
    Serial.begin(9600);            //Start serial
                                   communications.  Serial monitor
                                   must match this baud rate
    Wire.begin(SLAVE_ADDRESS);   //Start I2C link
    Wire.onReceive(receiveData); //Read data from EV3
    Serial.println("Ready!");
}
int val,flag=0,index=0;
byte d[]={10,11,12,13,14,15,16,17};   //Declare array to be sent
                                        to the Arduino
int i; //Declare loop increment
int red;   //Declare red color value
int green;   //Declare green color value
int blue;   //Declare blue color value

void loop()
{
 red = d[0]*2;   //Value from EV3 is 127 max, so double to set
                 to 254 max
 green = d[1]*2;   //Value from EV3 is 127 max, so double to set
                   to 254 max
 blue = d[2]*2;   //Value from EV3 is 127 max, so double to set
                  to 254 max
```

```
strip.begin();
for (int counter = 0; counter < 40; counter++){
strip.setPixelColor(counter,red,green,blue);
}
strip.show();
delay(100);
}

//Function for reading data.
void receiveData(int byteCount)
{
    i=0;
    while(Wire.available()>0)
        {
      val=Wire.read();
      d[i]=val;
      i = i + 1;
      flag=1;

    }

}
```

Using the Favorite Color Machine

Activating the Favorite Color Machine first turns off all the pixels in the NeoPixel Array, giving a blank display. Turning the motors for each color will increase the brightness for each constituent color, and mixing red/green/blue levels can generate any desired color. The user can dial in their favorite color and determine the associated red-green-blue components. The NeoPixel Shield can be set to be rather bright, so bright that it can be painful to look at up close.

Summary

This chapter showed using I2C to transfer data from the EV3 Intelligent Brick to the Arduino. Other chapters had the Arduino hosting a sensor to pass data to the EV3 Intelligent Brick, but the project presented here reversed this role to have the EV3 Intelligent Brick hosting the sensor. The example project involved used EV3 Medium Motors as rotation sensors to serve as adjustment knobs. Each of the three adjustment knobs controlled the setting of three constituent colors of red, green, and blue. The Arduino then read these color values to assign them for display on a NeoPixel Shield. Any desired color can be set by adjusting the red/green/blue values by rotation of the LEGO motors.

CHAPTER 12

Connecting MINDSTORMS to a Smartphone

Arduino shields can offer sophisticated functionality, such as the connection to a smartphone that will be explored in this chapter. The shield to accomplish this connection to a smartphone is the 1Sheeld+, shown in Figure 12-1. This shield features a Bluetooth connection between the smartphone and the Arduino, as well as an app for the smartphone to facilitate connection. Much of the functions and sensors built into a smartphone can be accessed through the Arduino and hence also to LEGO MINDSTORMS. Two projects are built in this chapter. The first, called the Tilt Mimic, will use a LEGO motor to tilt a Technic liftarm to the same angle of orientation of the phone. The second invention, called the Intrusion Monitor, uses a MINDSTORMS Ultrasonic Sensor as a trigger for a smartphone to take a picture and send a notification email message.

© Grady Koch 2020
G. Koch, *The LEGO Arduino Cookbook*, https://doi.org/10.1007/978-1-4842-6303-7_12

Figure 12-1. *The 1Sheeld+ sets up a Bluetooth communication link between the Arduino and a smartphone*

Mounting the 1Sheeld+

The 1Sheeld+ comes delivered with headers already installed, with no need to solder headers in place as was required in Chapters 10 and 11. Instead, the installation of the 1Sheeld+ proceeds by simply pressing it into place on the Arduino, as shown in Figure 12-2.

Figure 12-2. *The 1Sheeld+ mounts onto the Arduino*

Building the Tilt Mimic

The Tilt Mimic, shown in Figure 12-3, orients a Technic liftarm to the same angle measured by a smartphone. As the smartphone is tilted, an EV3 Medium Motor will go to the same angular orientation as the smartphone. Building instructions for the motor mount are shown after Figure 12-3.

Figure 12-3. *The Tilt Mimic rotates a Technic liftarm to the same angular orientation as a smartphone*

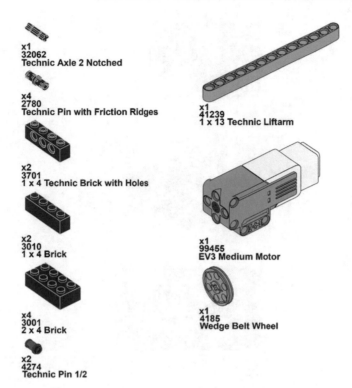

x1
32062
Technic Axle 2 Notched

x4
2780
Technic Pin with Friction Ridges

x1
41239
1 x 13 Technic Liftarm

x2
3701
1 x 4 Technic Brick with Holes

x2
3010
1 x 4 Brick

x1
99455
EV3 Medium Motor

x4
3001
2 x 4 Brick

x1
4185
Wedge Belt Wheel

x2
4274
Technic Pin 1/2

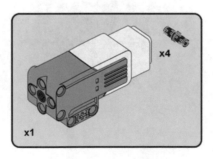

1

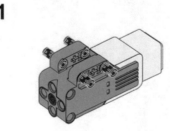

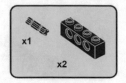

2

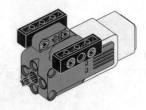

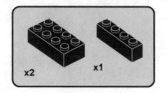

3

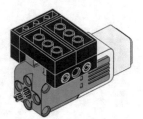

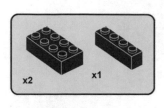

4

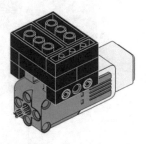

5

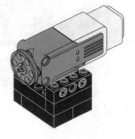

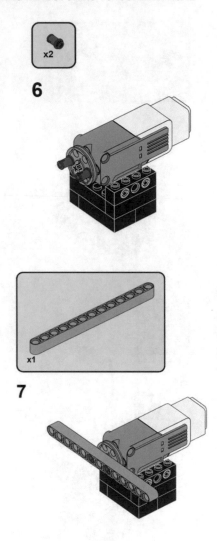

Wiring Connections for the Tilt Mimic

As with the shields used in Chapters 10 and 11, most of the wiring connections for the 1Sheeld+ are made by the headers of the 1Sheeld+ pressed into the Arduino. The remaining connection is an I2C link to pass data from the Arduino to the EV3 Intelligent Brick via the Breadboard

Connector—a diagram of this I2C wiring connection is given in Figure 12-4. An additional cable connection, diagrammed in Figure 12-5, connects the EV3 Intelligent Brick to an EV3 Medium Motor.

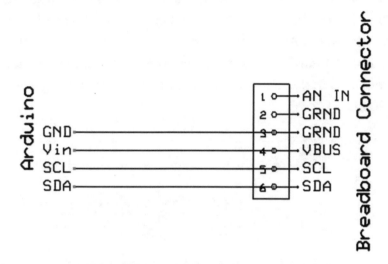

Figure 12-4. *Communication between the Arduino and the EV3 Intelligent Brick is by I2C*

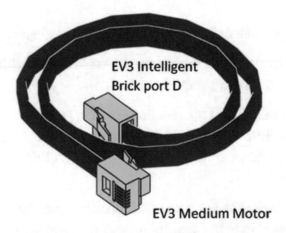

Figure 12-5. *An EV3 Medium Motor is connected to port D of the EV3 Intelligent Brick*

EV3 Code for the Tilt Mimic

The purpose of the EV3 code, shown in Figure 12-6, is to take in I2C data from the 1Sheeld+. This data is of the angular orientation of a smartphone, which the EV3 Intelligent Brick interprets into a setting to send to an EV3 Medium Motor. As the angle of the smartphone is changed, the EV3 motor will orient itself to the same angle. The result is that a Technic liftarm attached to the motor will always be parallel to the angle of the smartphone.

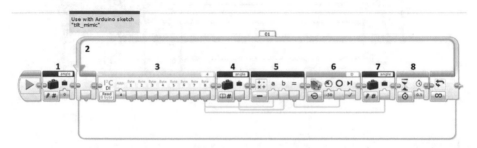

Figure 12-6. *The EV3 program for the Tilt Mimic reads in data over I2C connection*

Functions for each of the programming blocks in Figure 12-6 include

1. Variable Block: Loads a starting point for a variable called angle to a setpoint of 0.

2. Loop Block: Sets up an infinite loop to read in the orientation angle of the smartphone and continuously update the orientation of an EV3 motor.

3. I2C Block: Reads 1 byte of information from the I2C connection to the smartphone. Only 1 byte of the 8 possible bytes is used in this project.

4. Variable Block: Reads the value stored in the variable angle.

5. Math Block: Calculates the difference between the current and the prior orientation angle of the smartphone. If the smartphone has not changed in angle, the results of the calculation will be zero, meaning no change is made to the EV3 Medium Motor.

6. Medium Motor Block: Applies an angle of rotation to the motor, as calculated in block 5.

7. Variable Block: Updates the value of the variable angle to the current orientation of the smartphone.

8. Wait Block: Pauses for 0.1 second to avoid oversampling the I2C communication link.

Arduino Sketch for the Tilt Mimic

The Arduino sketch, shown in Listing 12-1, to monitor the angle of the smartphone makes use of libraries developed by 1Sheeld, available at www.1sheeld.com/downloads/.

Listing 12-1. The Arduino sketch for using the 1Sheeld+ should be run at the same time as the EV3 program "orientation"

```
/*--------------------------------------------------------

Orientation Shield Example

This example tilts a LEGO motor to the same angle measured for
Y-axis orientation of a smartphone.
```

Communication between EV3 Intelligent Brick and Arduino is by I2C
Connections:
1Sheeld to smartphone by bluetooth
EV3 Breadboard VBUS to Arduino VIN
EV3 Breadboard GRND (next to VBUS) to Arduino GND
EV3 Breadboard SCL to Arduino SCL
EV3 Breadboard SDA to Arduino SDA
EV3 cable between Breadboard Connector and Port 4 of EV3
Intelligent Brick

Use with EV3 program "orientation.ev3"

1Sheeld+ app on smartphone should be running shield for
Orientation

Remember to have 1Sheeld serial switch to SW to upload sketch,
then go to HW.

Arduino to EV3 connection modified from Dexter Industries post
www.dexterindustries.com/howto/connecting-ev3-arduino

```
----------------------------------------------------*/


#define CUSTOM_SETTINGS  //
#define INCLUDE_ORIENTATION_SENSOR_SHIELD  //

#include <OneSheeld.h>  //Call library for 1Sheeld

#include <Wire.h>  //Call library for I2C communications

#define SLAVE_ADDRESS 0x04  //I2C address for communicating
                            with EV3 Intelligent Brick.  Same
                            address should be in EV3 program.
```

```
byte c[]={10,11,12,13,14,15,16,17};   //Declare array that will
                                         be sent to EV3 Intelligent
                                         Brick.  Loaded with dummy
                                         values that can help
                                         de-bugging.

void setup()
{
  OneSheeld.begin(); //Start OneSheeld communications
  Wire.begin(SLAVE_ADDRESS);   //Start I2C communications
}

void loop()
{
  Serial.println(OrientationSensor.getY());   //Print
                                                orientation as
                                                diagnostic
  c[0] = OrientationSensor.getY();   //Store orientation in
                                       variable

  Wire.onRequest(sendData); //Send data to EV3
  delay(100);
}

//Function for sending data
void sendData()
{
  Wire.write(c,8); //c is the array of 8 bytes length.
}
```

In order to load the sketch onto the Arduino, a switch on the 1Sheeld+ board must be set into the "SW" position. The location of this switch is shown in Figure 12-7. After uploading the Arduino sketch, this switch should be placed into the "HW" position.

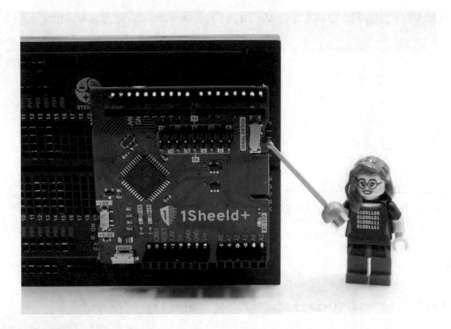

Figure 12-7. *The serial switch on the 1Sheeld+ must be set to "SW" when loading a sketch, then "HW" when running the sketch*

Setting Up the Smartphone for the Tilt Mimic

The 1Sheeld+ is set up and controlled by an app installed on a smartphone, available at www.1sheeld.com/downloads/. To initiate the Tilt Mimic, the functions of Email and Orientation are activated on this app. Screenshots of this setup are shown in Figures 12-8 to 12-12.

Figure 12-8. *Press "I have 1Sheeld Board" to begin the setup of the 1Sheeld app*

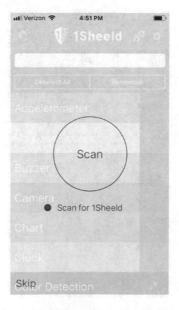

Figure 12-9. *Press inside the purple line of the "Scan" circle for the smartphone to find the 1Sheeld+ link*

Figure 12-10. *Press the name of the found 1Sheeld+ ("1Sheeld#NI" in this example) to establish the Bluetooth link between the smartphone and the 1Sheeld+*

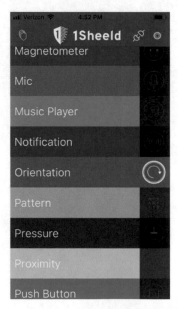

Figure 12-11. *Select the "Orientation" shield. Then press the small shield symbol in the upper left corner of the screen*

Figure 12-12. *Orientation measurements are displayed on the smartphone screen—the Y axis is used in the Tilt Mimic*

Running the Tilt Mimic

Before running the Tilt Mimic, the angle of the Technic liftarm connected to the EV3 Medium Motor should be set to horizontal—this can be done by simply taking hold of the liftarm and rotating it. This action sets the zero-degree starting point for tilt. To run the Tilt Mimic, three programs should be running:

- "orientation" on the EV3 Intelligent Brick

- "tilt_mimic" on the Arduino

- Orientation on the 1Sheeld+ app of the smartphone

A video of the Tilt Mimic in action can be seen on www.hightechlego.com.

Second 1Sheeld+ Project: Intrusion Monitor

The Intrusion Monitor, shown in Figure 12-13, detects when someone or something is within 50 cm of the EV3 Ultrasonic Sensor. When this proximity is triggered, the smartphone takes a photograph and sends an email notification. There are two parts to build: sensor mount and smartphone stand.

Figure 12-13. *The Intrusion Monitor detects objects with the EV3 Ultrasonic Sensor*

Building the Intrusion Monitor—Sensor Mount

The Ultrasonic Sensor Mount serves to hold the EV3 Ultrasonic Sensor, as built in the following steps.

x4
2780
Technic Pin with Friction Ridges

x2
3701
1 x 4 Technic Brick with Holes

x2
3010
1 x 4 Brick

x2
32316
1 x 5 Technic Liftarm

x1
45504
EV3 Ultrasonic Sensor

x4
3001
2 x 4 Brick

x2
6558
Long Technic Pin with Friction Ridges

1

2

3

4

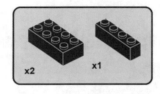

5

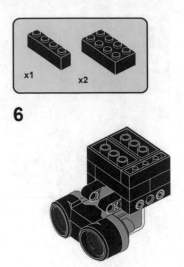

Building the Intrusion Monitor— Smartphone Stand

The smartphone stand gives a place for the phone to rest, with the camera facing in the same direction as the EV3 Ultrasonic Sensor. Building instructions are given as follows.

x10
2780
Technic Pin with Friction Ridges

x2
3894
1 x 6 Technic Brick with Holes

x2
32009
Double Bent Liftarm

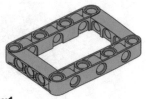

x1
64179
5 x 7 Open Center Frame Liftarm

x2
32062
Technic Axle 2 Notched

x2
32184
Axle and Pin Connector

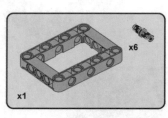

x6

x1

1

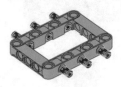

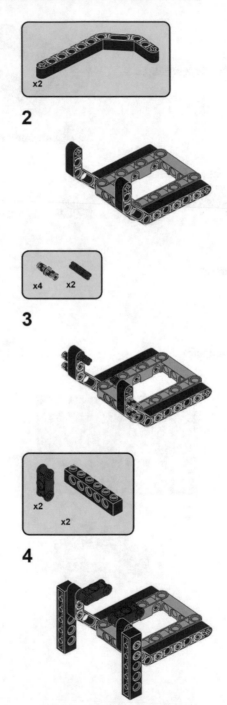

2

3

4

Wiring the Intrusion Monitor

The control signal from the EV3 Intelligent Brick to the Arduino is a digital pulse, created by adapting a motor control signal in the EV3 programming environment. This digital pulse indicates when the Arduino should initiate actions, in this case, to have the smartphone (via the 1Sheeld+) take a photograph and send an email. Figure 12-14 shows the circuit and wiring connections to make for the digital pulse control signal. I2C is not used here for this communication link because doing so creates signal conflicts with the 1Sheeld+. The voltage taken from AN IN on the Breadboard Connector has a voltage level too high to work with the Arduino, posing a risk of damaging the Arduino. So a pair of resistors is used in a voltage divider circuit to lower the voltage to about 4 volts.

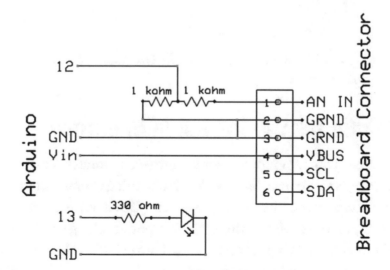

Figure 12-14. *Wiring for the Intrusion Monitor includes two circuits: a voltage divider to input to Arduino pin 12 and an LED on Arduino pin 13*

The circuit of Figure 12-14 also includes an LED connected to pin 13 of the Arduino to give an indication of when an event has been triggered by the EV3 Intelligent Brick. The LED will light up for the duration of the pulse created by the EV3 program, providing a confirmation that the setup is working. The Breadboard Connector is then connected with the EV3 Intelligent Brick port A, as per the diagram in Figure 12-15. Also shown in Figure 12-15 is another EV3 connection between the Intelligent Brick port 4 and the Ultrasonic Sensor.

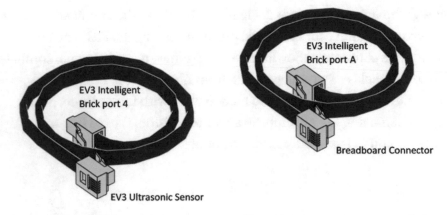

Figure 12-15. *EV3 cables connect to the Ultrasonic Sensor and the Breadboard Connector*

EV3 Code for the Intrusion Monitor

The function of the EV3 program for the Intrusion Monitor, shown in Figure 12-16, is to create a digital pulse if something comes within a certain distance of the Ultrasonic Sensor. The digital pulse is created by repurposing an Unregulated Motor block. A power setting of 100% on this block will create a 7.5V signal on the AN IN pin of the breakout board. The voltage drops to zero when the motor is shut off by the Unregulated Motor block.

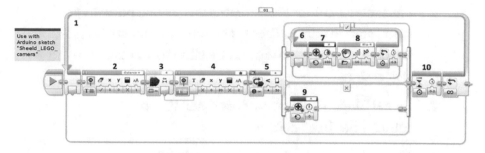

Figure 12-16. *The EV3 program for the Intrusion Monitor uses an Ultrasonic Sensor as a trigger*

Steps in the EV3 code include

1. Loop Block: Creates an infinite repetition of monitoring the output of the EV3 Ultrasonic Sensor.

2. Display Block: Prints a label on the EV3 Intelligent Brick's front panel display as a reminder of the quantity being measured.

3. Ultrasonic Sensor Block: Takes a distance reading from the EV3 Ultrasonic Sensor.

4. Display Block: Prints the measurement results of block 3 to the front panel display.

5. Switch Block: Based on the EV3 Ultrasonic Sensor, executes blocks 6–8 to generate the digital pulse and play a sound if an object is found within 50 cm of the sensor. Otherwise, if nothing is detected, block 9 is run to reset the output to 0 V.

6. Loop Block: Keeps blocks within it active for 0.5 seconds.

7. Unregulated Motor Block: Turns on a digital pulse connected to port A. There is no motor connected to port A, but rather a wire connection to access the digital signal.

8. Sound Block: Gives an audible signal that an intruder has been detected.

9. Unregulated Motor Block: Ensures that the digital pulse is off, in the event that nothing has been detected by the EV3 Ultrasonic Sensor.

10. Wait Block: Pauses operation for 0.2 seconds to avoid signals being confused between the Arduino and the EV3 Intelligent Brick.

Arduino Sketch for the Intrusion Monitor

When triggered by a digital pulse input on pin 12, the Arduino executes commands to the 1Sheeld+ to have the smartphone take a photograph and send a notification email. The sketch is shown in Listing 12-2.

Listing 12-2. The Arduino sketch for using the 1Sheeld+ for the Intrusion Monitor should be run at the same time as the EV3 program "ultrasonic_trigger"

```
/*--------------------------------------------------------

LEGO Intrusion Monitor
Takes a digital trigger on pin 12 to have the 1Sheeld+ take a
picture and send a notification email.
```

Connections:

EV3 Breadboard Connector VBUS to Arduino VIN

EV3 Breadboard Connector GRND (next to VBUS) to Arduino GND

EV3 Breadboard Connector GRND wired together with jumper wire

EV3 Breadboard Connector AN IN to two 1-kohm resistors in series.

Other end of series resistors to Arduino GND

Arduino Pin 12 to joint of series resistors

Arduino Pin 13 to 330-ohm resistor in series with LED

Other end of LED to Arduino GND

This sketch is used in conjuction with EV3 code "ultrasonic_ trigger.ev3"

1Sheeld+ app on smartphone should be running sheelds for Email and Camera

Sections of code taken from examples provided by 1Sheeld

```
------------------------------------------------------*/

#define CUSTOM_SETTINGS //
#define INCLUDE_CAMERA_SHIELD  //
#define INCLUDE_EMAIL_SHIELD  //

#include <OneSheeld.h> //Call library for 1Sheeld

int buttonPin = 12; //Set input pin, connected to EV3
Intelligent Brick
int ledPin = 13; //Set output pin, connected to LED

void setup()
{

  OneSheeld.begin(); //Start 1Sheeld communications
  pinMode(buttonPin,INPUT); //Set button pin as input
  pinMode(ledPin,OUTPUT); //Sets LED pin as output
}
```

```
void loop()
{
  if(digitalRead(buttonPin) == HIGH) //Checks the digital input
                                 state
  {
    digitalWrite(ledPin,HIGH); //Turn on LED
    Camera.frontCapture(); //Take a picture with front camera
    Email.send("type_your_address_here@gmail.com","Intruder!",
    "I took a picture of intruder!"); //Send email
    OneSheeld.delay(10000);  //Wait for 10 seconds
  }
  else
  {
    digitalWrite(ledPin,LOW);//Turn off LED
  }

}
```

Setting Up the Smartphone for the Intrusion Monitor

The app for 1Sheeld+ on the smartphone needs to have shields activated for Email and Camera, as shown in Figure 12-17. The steps prior to selecting these two shields are the same as for the Tilt Mimic in Figures 12-8 to 12-10. The Email function on the 1Sheeld+ only works with Gmail accounts, so such an account may have to be created at www.gmail. google.com.

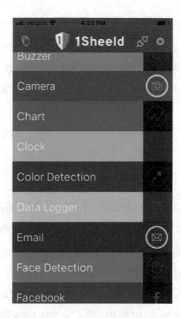

Figure 12-17. *Shields for Camera and Email should be selected on the 1Sheeld+ app*

Running the Intrusion Monitor

Three programs should be running for the activation of the Intrusion Monitor:

- "ultrasonic_trigger" on the EV3 Intelligent Brick

- "Sheeld_LEGO_camera" on the Arduino

- Camera and Email on the 1Sheeld+ app of the smartphone

Notice must also be taken that the switch on the 1Sheeld+ should be in the "HW" position. When an object gets within 50 cm of the EV3 Ultrasonic Trigger, the sound should play on the EV3 Intelligent Brick, and the LED connected to Arduino pin 13 should light up. The smartphone, with the 1Sheeld+ app running, should show a notification at the bottom of the screen that an email message has been generated. There's then a delay of about 7 seconds before the smartphone takes a picture, which shows up as a thumbnail image at the bottom of the smartphone screen. Photographs are stored on the smartphone at the same location as all of the photos on the phone.

Summary

This chapter used an Arduino shield to interface LEGO MINDSTORMS with a smartphone. The functionality of the smartphone can be accessed through MINDSTORMS, including the many sensors imbedded in the phone and communications. Two projects were built, using the 1Sheeld+, to demonstrate the MINDSTORMS/smartphone interface. The first project tilted a LEGO motor to the same angular orientation of the smartphone. The second project used the capability to access multiple smartphone functions, in this case email and camera. A LEGO EV3 Ultrasonic Sensor served as a sensor to detect intruders, which when triggered had the smartphone take a photograph and send a notification email. The 1Sheeld+ has many other functions that can be explored for even more sophisticated inventions, such as the use of voice recognition or cellular telephone calls.

Appendix

Parts used in this book are organized in the following by chapter. Some chapters involve only software, and so these chapters do not have an associated parts list. LEGO parts are listed in tables, and non-LEGO parts are given in bullet lists along with sources for their purchase. Aside from the parts listed, several tools are used, including

- Soldering iron and solder

- Diagonal cutters

- Wire strippers

Parts Used in Chapter 1 for the LEGO Arduino Workstation
The LEGO Arduino Workstation uses the LEGO parts summarized in Table A-1. Non-LEGO parts include

- An Arduino Uno+breadboard shield+LEGO mounting, either in the form of

    - STEMTera: Available at `www.sparkfun.com`, `www.amazon.com`, `www.digikey.com`, or `www.mouser.com`
  or
    - An assembled stack consisting of

        - Arduino Uno: Available at many online electronics stores

        - Proto Shield: Available at `www.adafruit.com`, `www.mouser.com`, and `www.digikey.com`

        - LEGO Adapter: Available at `www.shapeways.com` as "Arduino UNO LEGO adapter"

© Grady Koch 2020
G. Koch, *The LEGO Arduino Cookbook*, https://doi.org/10.1007/978-1-4842-6303-7

- Breadboard Connector Kit: Available at
  www.mindsensors.com

Table A-1. *LEGO parts used to build the LEGO Arduino Workstation*

Part Number	Part Name	Quantity
2780	Technic Pin with Friction Ridges	4
3001	2 x 4 Brick	6
2456	2 x 6 Brick	4
3895	1 x 12 Technic Brick with Holes	2
30072	12 x 24 Brick	4
95646	EV3 Intelligent Brick	1
55805	Connector Cable	1

Parts Used in Chapter 5 for the LEGO Metal Detector

The LEGO Metal Detector uses the LEGO Arduino Workstation of Chapter 1 for the first implementation described. LEGO parts for the handheld version of the LEGO Metal Detector are described in Table A-2. Non-LEGO parts include

- Grove 2-Channel Inductive Sensor made by Seeed Studio, available at www.seeedstudio.com or electronics parts distributors www.robotshop.com and www.mouser.com

- Grove Wrapper made by Seeed Studio, available at the same sources for the sensor

- 4.7-kΩ resistor, ¼ watt (or higher)

- 1-µF ceramic capacitor

- Jumper wires

Table A-2. *LEGO parts used to build the LEGO Metal Detector, in addition to the parts for the LEGO Arduino Workstation*

Part Number	Part Name	Quantity
2780	Technic Pin with Friction Ridges	3
3703	1 x 16 Technic Brick with Holes	1
4274	Technic Pin 1/2	8

Parts Used in Chapter 6 for Programmable LEDs

The Programmable LEDs project uses the LEGO Arduino Workstation of Chapter 1, plus a brick to hold the LED array as identified in Table A-3. Non-LEGO parts include

- Qwiic LED Stick made by SparkFun and available at www.sparkfun.com

- M3 screws (at least 16 mm long) and nuts (two of each) for mounting the Qwiic LED Stick

- 4.7-kΩ resistor, ¼ watt (or higher)

- 10-kΩ resistor, ¼ watt (or higher)

- 1-kΩ resistor, ¼ watt (or higher)

- 1-μF ceramic capacitor

- Jumper wires

Table A-3. *LEGO part used to build Programmable LEDs, in addition to the parts for the LEGO Arduino Workstation*

Part Number	Part Name	Quantity
3703	1 x 14 Technic Brick with Holes	1

Parts Used in Chapter 8 for the LEGO Lidar

The LEGO Lidar uses the LEGO Arduino Workstation of Chapter 1 as a platform, plus the additional LEGO parts described in Table A-4. Non-LEGO parts include

- LIDAR-Lite v3 made by Garmin, available at www.sparkfun.com, www.robotshop.com, www.digikey.com, and www.mouser.com

- 1-kΩ resistor, ¼ watt (or higher)

- Jumper wires

- Cyanoacrylate glue such as Gorilla Glue or Super Glue

- Vision Subsystem v5 made by Mindsensors.com

- 120-degree field of view M12 lens made by Arducam and available at www.robotshop.com and www.amazon.com

Table A-4. *LEGO parts used to build the LEGO Lidar, in addition to the parts for the LEGO Arduino Workstation*

Part Number	Part Name	Quantity
2780	Technic Pin with Friction Ridges	2
32054	Technic Pin with Stop Bush	2
3701	1 x 4 Technic Brick with Holes	1
3894	1 x 6 Technic Brick with Holes	1
3001	2 x 4 Brick	1
3702	1 x 8 Technic Brick with Holes	2
3034	2 x 8 Plate	1
6558	Long Technic Pin with Friction Ridges	4
48989	Technic 4-Pin Connector	1

(continued)

Table A-4. (*continued*)

Part Number	Part Name	Quantity
64179	5 x 7 Open Center Frame Liftarm	1
95658	EV3 Large Motor	1
55805	Connector Cable	1

Parts Used in Chapter 9 for the LEGO Weather Station

The LEGO Weather Station uses the LEGO Arduino Workstation of Chapter 1 as a platform, plus the LEGO parts identified in Table A-5. Non-LEGO parts include

- Atmospheric Sensor made by SparkFun and available at www.sparkfun.com

- M3 screw (at least 16 mm long) and nut for mounting the Atmospheric Sensor

- Jumper wires

Table A-5. *LEGO parts used to build the LEGO Weather Station, in addition to the parts for the LEGO Arduino Workstation*

Part Number	Part Name	Quantity
2780	Technic Pin with Friction Ridges	2
3701	1 x 4 Technic Brick with Holes	1
2730	1 x 10 Technic Brick with Holes	1
64178	5 x 11 Open Center Frame Liftarm	1
6558	Long Technic Pin with Friction Ridges	2
95650	EV3 Color Sensor	1
55805	Connector Cable	1

Parts Used in Chapter 10 for the LEGO Spectrum Analyzer

The LEGO Spectrum Analyzer uses the LEGO Arduino Workstation of Chapter 1 as a platform. Motorized dancing mechanisms were adapted from projects in the *The LEGO MINDSTORMS EV3 Idea Book* written by Yoshihito Isogawa. Non-LEGO parts include

- Spectrum Shield made by SparkFun and available at www.sparkfun.com

- Headers for the Spectrum Shield, also available at www.sparkfun.com

- LED Array made by Mindsensors.com

Parts Used in Chapter 11 for the Favorite Color Machine

The LEGO Favorite Color Machine uses the LEGO Arduino Workstation of Chapter 1 as a platform, plus the LEGO parts identified in Table A-6. Non-LEGO parts include

- NeoPixel Shield made by Adafruit and available at www.adafruit.com, www.sparkfun.com, and www.amazon.com

Table A-6. *LEGO parts used to build the Favorite Color Machine, in addition to the parts for the LEGO Arduino Workstation*

Part Number	Part Name	Quantity
2780	Technic Pin with Friction Ridges	12
3701	1 x 4 Technic Brick with Holes	6
56145	Wheel	3
44309	Tire	3
3713	Technic Bush	3
99455	EV3 Medium Motor	3
99008	Technic Axle 4 with Center Stop	3
55805	Connector Cable	3

Parts Used in Chapter 12 for Connecting MINDSTORMS to a Smartphone

Connecting MINDSTORMS to a smartphone uses the LEGO Arduino Workstation of Chapter 1 as a platform, plus the LEGO parts identified in Tables A-7 and A-8. Non-LEGO parts include

- 1Sheeld+ made by 1Sheeld and available at www.adafruit.com, www.sparkfun.com, www.newark.com, and www.amazon.com

Table A-7. *LEGO parts used to build the Tilt Mimic, in addition to the parts for the LEGO Arduino Workstation*

Part Number	Part Name	Quantity
2780	Technic Pin with Friction Ridges	4
3701	1 x 4 Technic Brick with Holes	2
32062	Technic Axle 2 Notched	1
3010	1 x 4 Brick	2
3713	2 x 4 Brick	4
4274	Technic Pin ½	2
41239	1 x 13 Technic Liftarm	1
4185	Wedge Belt Wheel	1
99455	EV3 Medium Motor	1
55805	Connector Cable	1

Table A-8. *LEGO parts used to build the Intrusion Monitor, in addition to the parts for the LEGO Arduino Workstation*

Part Number	Part Name	Quantity
2780	Technic Pin with Friction Ridges	4
3701	1 x 4 Technic Brick with Holes	2
3010	1 x 4 Brick	2
3713	2 x 4 Brick	4
32316	1 x 5 Technic Liftarm	2
6558	Long Technic Pin with Friction Ridges	2
99455	EV3 Ultrasonic Sensor	1
55805	Connector Cable	1

Index

A, B, C, D

E

F, G, H

I, J, K

© Grady Koch 2020
G. Koch, *The LEGO Arduino Cookbook*, https://doi.org/10.1007/978-1-4842-6303-7

T, U, V, W, X, Y, Z

Printed in the United States
By Bookmasters